# The World of...
# English
## SATs Revision

## Alison Head

Good day. I'm Sir Ralph Witherbottom. I'm an accomplished inventor, a dashing discoverer and an enthusiastic entrepreneur.

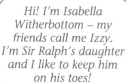

Hi! I'm Isabella Witherbottom – my friends call me Izzy. I'm Sir Ralph's daughter and I like to keep him on his toes!

And they both keep me on my toes! How do you do? I'm Max, the butler, at your service.

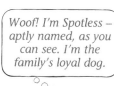

Woof! I'm Spotless – aptly named, as you can see. I'm the family's loyal dog.

# Contents

**Golden Rules** . . . . . . . . . . . . . . . . . . . . . . . . . . . **4**
Spelling rules

**Family Tree** . . . . . . . . . . . . . . . . . . . . . . . . . . . **6**
Strategies for tricky spellings

**Too Much Stuff** . . . . . . . . . . . . . . . . . . . . . . . . **8**
Nouns and pronouns

**Reporting the Action** . . . . . . . . . . . . . . . . . . .**10**
Verbs and adverbs

**The Perfect Place** . . . . . . . . . . . . . . . . . . . . . .**12**
Adjectives

**Cracking the Code** . . . . . . . . . . . . . . . . . . . . . .**14**
Punctuating sentences

**He Said What?** . . . . . . . . . . . . . . . . . . . . . . . . .**16**
Punctuating speech, direct and reported speech

**Short Cuts** . . . . . . . . . . . . . . . . . . . . . . . . . . . .**18**
Apostrophes, its and it's

**A Crabby Connection** . . . . . . . . . . . . . . . . . . . .**20**
Clauses, simple and complex sentences

**One Slice at a Time** . . . . . . . . . . . . . . . . . . . . .**22**
Paragraphs

**Lost and Found** . . . . . . . . . . . . . . . . . . . . . . . .**24**
Tenses, irregular verbs

**Brainstorm** . . . . . . . . . . . . . . . . . . . . . . . . . . .**26**
Spelling and grammar

**Revise Time** . . . . . . . . . . . . . . . . . . . . . . . . . . .**28**

**Hunting High and Low** . . . . . . . . . . . . . . . . . .**30**
Reading: information retrieval

**Story Detective** . . . . . . . . . . . . . . . . . . . . . . . .**32**
Reading: inference and deduction

**Precious Preparations** . . . . . . . . . . . . . . . . . .**34**
Reading: fiction

**Reading Rules** . . . . . . . . . . . . . . . . . . . . . . . . .**36**
Reading: non-fiction

**Secrets in the Sand** . . . . . . . . . . . . . . . . . . . . .**38**
Reading: poetry

**Brainstorm** . . . . . . . . . . . . . . . . . . . . . . . . . . .**40**
Reading skills

**Revise Time** . . . . . . . . . . . . . . . . . . . . . . . . . . .**42**

**Recipe for a Good Story** . . . . . . . . . . . . . . . . . **44**
  Writing fiction: structure

**Puzzled About Planning?** . . . . . . . . . . . . . . . . **46**
  Writing a plan

**Snack Attack** . . . . . . . . . . . . . . . . . . . . . . **48**
  Openings and endings

**Blast from the Past** . . . . . . . . . . . . . . . . . . **50**
  Writing about characters

**Picture Perfect** . . . . . . . . . . . . . . . . . . . . **52**
  Writing about setting

**The Sorcerer's Apprentice** . . . . . . . . . . . . . . . **54**
  Choosing and using language

**Tricks of the Trade** . . . . . . . . . . . . . . . . . . **56**
  Techniques to hook your reader

**All Dressed Up** . . . . . . . . . . . . . . . . . . . . . **58**
  Genre

**Brainstorm** . . . . . . . . . . . . . . . . . . . . . . . **60**
  Writing fiction

**Revise Time** . . . . . . . . . . . . . . . . . . . . . . . **62**

**Lessons from Lists** . . . . . . . . . . . . . . . . . . . **64**
  Writing instructions

**A Dog's Day** . . . . . . . . . . . . . . . . . . . . . . . **66**
  Journalistic writing

**Party Planning** . . . . . . . . . . . . . . . . . . . . . **68**
  Advertising

**Bright Sparks** . . . . . . . . . . . . . . . . . . . . . . **70**
  Letters

**The Cream Cake Caper** . . . . . . . . . . . . . . . . . . **72**
  Chronological reports and recounts

**A Dog's Life** . . . . . . . . . . . . . . . . . . . . . . **74**
  Non-chronological reports

**For Your Eyes Only** . . . . . . . . . . . . . . . . . . . **76**
  Writing a diary

**Bus Stop Bust-up** . . . . . . . . . . . . . . . . . . . . **78**
  Balanced arguments

**Brainstorm** . . . . . . . . . . . . . . . . . . . . . . . **80**
  Writing non-fiction

**Revise Time** . . . . . . . . . . . . . . . . . . . . . . . **82**

**SATs Style Questions** . . . . . . . . . **84**
**Glossary** . . . . . . . . . . . . . . . . . **92**
**Answers** . . . . . . . . . . . . . . . . . **94**

# Golden Rules

Isabella Witherbottom was looking through the records of Sir Ralph Witherbottom's latest experiment.

"How can you possibly read these notes, Dad? Your writing's so messy, and what are all these words you've circled?"

"That was my first draft. I kept getting my **suffixes** wrong, so I went through and circled all my mistakes so I could correct them in the second draft."

Investigations into alchemy.

Tuesday

I have been mixing the chemicals together in (variing) proportions, (takeing) care to note the exact weight of each chemical used.

The first mixture I (tryed) produced the (prettyest) pink liquid I have ever seen. My second attempt matched its (prettyness) but neither looked anything like gold.

"What is a suffix, Dad?" asked Isabella.

"Suffixes are groups of letters you can add to the ends of words to change their meaning," explained Sir Ralph. "They help you build lots of new words, but you can't always just add them to your **root word**, without changing its spelling first.

take + ing = taking

care + ed = cared

"If your root word ends in e, for instance, you normally have to take off the e before you add a suffix that starts with a **vowel**.

"With suffixes that start with a **consonant**, on the other hand, you can leave the e."

"Great, Dad. Are there any exceptions I need to know about?"

"Just a few, Izzy. Words like *seeing*, *freeing* and *being* all keep their e when you add *ing*."

care + less = careless

live + ly = lively

"OK, but what about the word *prettyness*? That looks wrong to me. Is it?" asked Isabella.

"Well spotted, lots of root words end in a consonant followed by *y*. You can usually just add the suffix *ing* to these words, but to add the suffixes *ness*, *er*, *ed*, or *est* to words ending in *y*, you need to change the final *y* of the root word to an *i*."

carry + er = carrier

fry + ed = fried

"So much to learn!" complained Isabella. "Well, at least there are rules to help, I suppose. Shame they can't help your handwriting, though!"

*Sir Ralph's notebooks make about as much sense to me as these hieroglyphics!*

## Top Tips!

The word *full* is a really useful suffix for making **adjectives**, but remember that when it is used as a suffix, it only has one *l*.

beauty + full = beautiful

# Did you know?

The ancient Egyptians didn't have to worry about spelling. Each of their hieroglyphic symbols stood for a thing, an idea or a sound, and they spelt words exactly the way they sounded. If, however, you think that sounds easy, it's worth remembering that they had hundreds of different symbols and often wrote back to front!

# Family Tree

Sir Ralph Witherbottom showed Isabella a large, dusty book. "I'm tracing our family tree. Do you know, there have been scientists and inventors in our family for four hundred years? Don't you think I look like this portrait of one of our ancestors? Very distinguished!"

"That's all very interesting, Dad, but I was hoping you could help me with my spellings," pleaded Isabella.

"Well, funnily enough, Izzy, this family album might just be able to help you with that."

"How could it possibly do that, Dad?" asked Isabella, looking very doubtful.

"Well, Izzy, you see just as there are similarities between different members of our family, there are similarities between members of **word families** too. Word families are groups of words that share the same root, **prefix** or **suffix**. Being able to spell one word in a family will help you to spell the others.

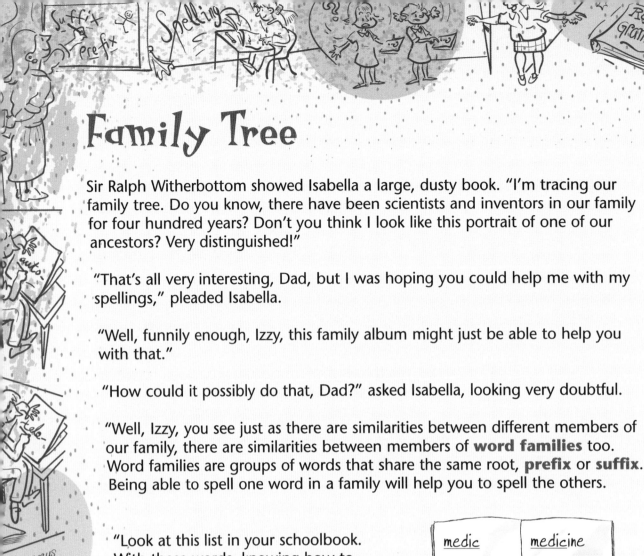

"Look at this list in your schoolbook. With these words, knowing how to spell the **root word** on the left, helps you to spell the word in the right-hand column correctly."

| | |
|---|---|
| medic | medicine |
| govern | government |
| cycle | bicycle |

"Look at this list too, Dad. These words all contain prefixes or suffixes that aren't spelt quite how they sound. So if I learn to spell the prefix or suffix, I guess I'll be able to spell a lot of other words too."

| | |
|---|---|
| photograph | telegraph |
| telephone | television |
| audition | audible |

"That's right, Izzy. Word families can also help you to spell words that contain unstressed **vowels**. These are vowels that we either don't say at all, or don't pronounce clearly, when we say a word.

| | |
|---|---|
| jeweller | jewellery |
| confer | conference |
| origin | original |

"So playing word detective can help you solve spelling puzzles, just like tracing a family tree," explained Sir Ralph, with some satisfaction.

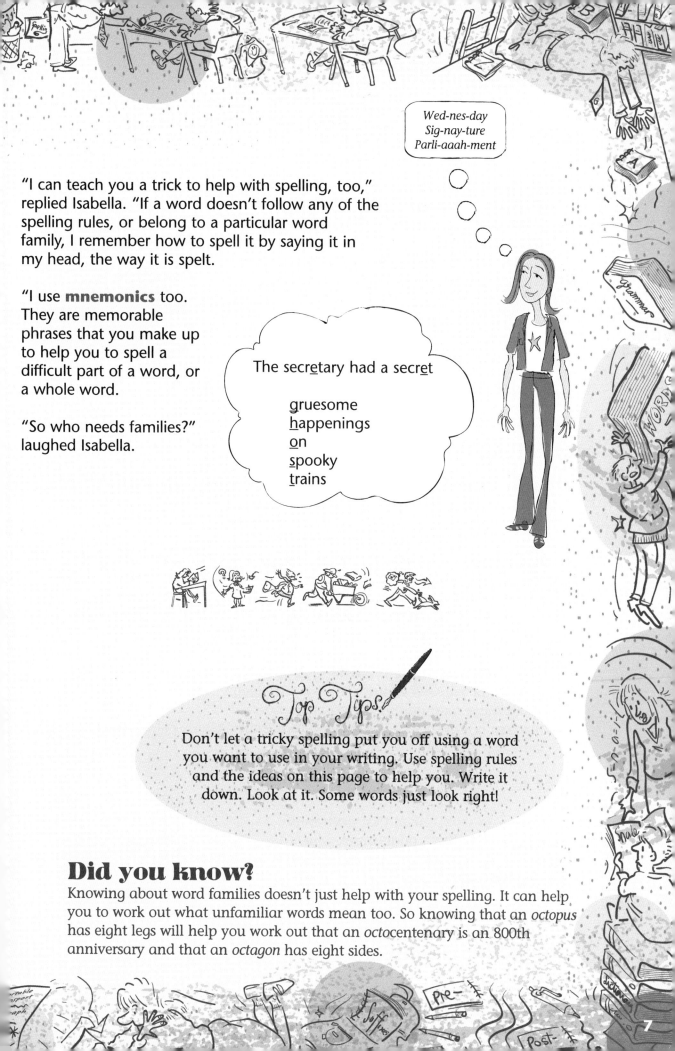

Wed-nes-day
Sig-nay-ture
Parli-aaah-ment

"I can teach you a trick to help with spelling, too," replied Isabella. "If a word doesn't follow any of the spelling rules, or belong to a particular word family, I remember how to spell it by saying it in my head, the way it is spelt.

"I use **mnemonics** too. They are memorable phrases that you make up to help you to spell a difficult part of a word, or a whole word.

"So who needs families?" laughed Isabella.

The sec<u>re</u>tary had a secr<u>et</u>

<u>g</u>ruesome
<u>h</u>appenings
<u>o</u>n
<u>s</u>pooky
<u>t</u>rains

## Top Tips!

Don't let a tricky spelling put you off using a word you want to use in your writing. Use spelling rules and the ideas on this page to help you. Write it down. Look at it. Some words just look right!

## Did you know?

Knowing about word families doesn't just help with your spelling. It can help you to work out what unfamiliar words mean too. So knowing that an *octopus* has eight legs will help you work out that an *octocentenary* is an 800th anniversary and that an *octagon* has eight sides.

# Too Much Stuff

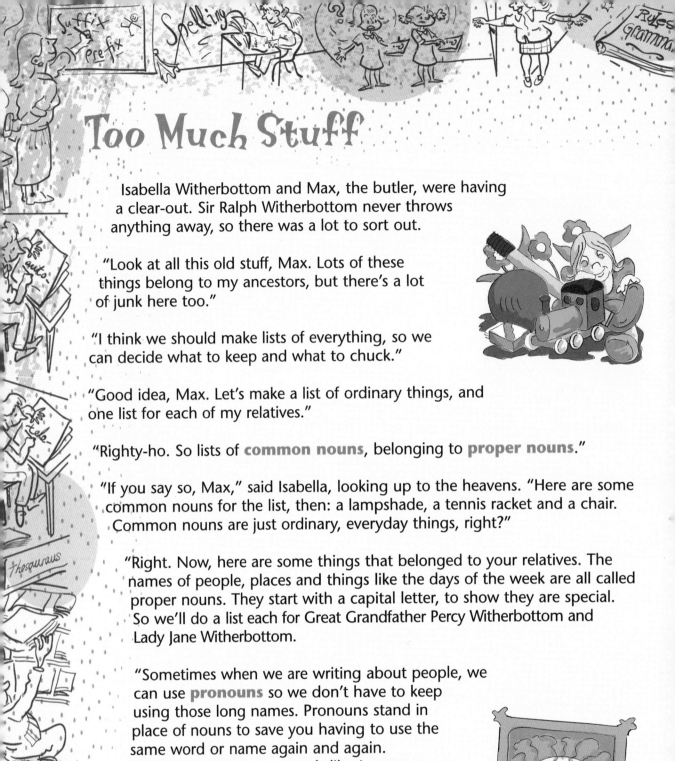

Isabella Witherbottom and Max, the butler, were having a clear-out. Sir Ralph Witherbottom never throws anything away, so there was a lot to sort out.

"Look at all this old stuff, Max. Lots of these things belong to my ancestors, but there's a lot of junk here too."

"I think we should make lists of everything, so we can decide what to keep and what to chuck."

"Good idea, Max. Let's make a list of ordinary things, and one list for each of my relatives."

"Righty-ho. So lists of **common nouns**, belonging to **proper nouns**."

"If you say so, Max," said Isabella, looking up to the heavens. "Here are some common nouns for the list, then: a lampshade, a tennis racket and a chair. Common nouns are just ordinary, everyday things, right?"

"Right. Now, here are some things that belonged to your relatives. The names of people, places and things like the days of the week are all called proper nouns. They start with a capital letter, to show they are special. So we'll do a list each for Great Grandfather Percy Witherbottom and Lady Jane Witherbottom.

"Sometimes when we are writing about people, we can use **pronouns** so we don't have to keep using those long names. Pronouns stand in place of nouns to save you having to use the same word or name again and again. Personal pronouns are words like *I, me, we,* or *he.*

"So we can say 'Look at that portrait of Lady Jane. *She* has a huge nose'. Much quicker than using her name twice, and it sounds better too."

"Don't let Dad hear you say that," said Isabella. "He's very proud of the Witherbottom nose!"

Common nouns? In my attic? Surely not! Only the very best nouns for the Witherbottoms!

"These old toys, on the other hand, would be described by **collective nouns**. Collective nouns describe a group of nouns, so we have a *flock* of little toy sheep, a *pack* of cards and a *bunch* of silk flowers.

"Just look at all this stuff, Izzy! Imagine all the memories, the happiness and sadness that went with them. Those are nouns too, you know. Feelings or ideas are called **abstract nouns**. You can't see them, but they are still nouns."

"You big softy, Max. Aitchoo! What about dust? I suppose that's a common noun, is it? It's certainly common enough around here, anyway. Let's get some fresh air."

## Top Tips!

Pronouns usually only have a capital letter if they appear at the start of a **sentence**. The only exception is *I*, which is always a capital letter.

## Did you know?

Nouns can be **singular**, which means one, or **plural**, which means more than one. To make a noun plural, you can usually just add *s*, but with words that end with *sh* or a hissing sound, you add *es*.
*brush + s = brushes*
And with words that end in *y*, you have to take off the *y*, and add *ies*.
*baby + s = babies*

# Reporting the Action

Isabella had been asked to report on a hockey match between her school and a neighbouring school. The trouble was, when she came to write the story, she found there was an awful lot about people running after the ball and hitting it and, after a while, the report was starting to sound really boring. Max loved reading the sports pages, so she went to ask him for help.

Chloe ran after the ball and hit it towards Dawn. Dawn hit it to Erin who ran on towards the goal, dribbling the ball.

"You know what the problem is, Izzy? Your **verbs**," said Max. "Verbs are being or doing words and every **sentence** has to have one. Being verbs are things like *I am* or *I have*. Doing verbs are all about actions, so you'll need lots of them in your report.

"You may need to write a lot about running about, but you don't have to use the verb *run* every time. You could choose powerful verbs that say more about how the player was running, like *jog*, *dash* or *sprint*. Powerful verbs really bring your writing to life and grab your readers' attention."

Call that chasing the ball? If they'd let dogs play hockey, I'd show them.

"Great, Max, thanks. What else do I need to know about verbs?"

"Well, some verbs are **active** and some are **passive**. In the sentence *Chloe smacked the ball*, *smacked* is active, because it describes what Chloe did. But in the sentence *The ball was smacked by Chloe*, the verb is passive, because it describes what happened to the ball. On the whole, active verbs are better, because they are more powerful, but the odd passive verb is OK, to add variety."

"Great, but even with all these powerful verbs, I'm still going to have to use the same one more than once. How else can I describe what happened on the pitch?"

"**Adverbs** are great for that. They describe verbs and can really help to paint a picture for your readers. So a player might run *swiftly* or *ploddingly*, and your team might win the match *decisively* or *narrowly*. Adverbs can also describe where and when something happens. Team up a powerful verb with a great adverb and you can't go wrong."

Isabella paused for a minute, scribbled something down, then passed it to Max saying, "So I could write it like this..."

> Chloe dashed after the ball and smacked it towards Dawn. Dawn knocked it backwards to Erin who immediately sprinted on towards the goal, dribbling the ball swiftly.

"Well done, Izzy. With verbs and adverbs like that, your readers will feel like they're watching the match themselves."

## Top Tips

Collect really powerful verbs and adverbs from your reading, or from a **thesaurus**, to use in your own writing. Read through what you've written and try replacing any boring verbs with more powerful ones. Try adding adverbs too.

## Did you know?

Verbs describe what **nouns** are doing. The form of the verb you need may change, depending on whether the noun is **singular** or **plural**. You need to be especially careful if you are writing about the **present tense** – that is, things that are happening now. One player *runs* after the ball, but two players *run* after the ball.

# The Perfect Place

Historical . Cultural
Peaceful

EXCITING
Lively
MODERN

Sir Ralph and Isabella decided to book a summer holiday and sent Max off to collect some brochures. While he was gone, they each thought about the kind of place they'd like to stay in. They both knew exactly what they wanted, but were finding it hard to agree on anything.

By the time Max returned with the brochures, Sir Ralph and Isabella were sulking. They had compared their lists and were sure they would never find a place that would suit them both.

"There's sure to be the right place in here somewhere," Max assured them. "When you were thinking about the place you'd like to go to, you probably came up with a list of **adjectives**. Adjectives describe **nouns**.

"These holiday brochures use adjectives to describe the different resorts and hotels. Without them, all the hotels would sound the same. Some of the adjectives are used to compare different places. For example, they say that this hotel is *closer to the beach than many of the resort's other hotels*, but this one is *quieter than many of its neighbours*. These are called **comparative adjectives**.

"Other adjectives describe the fullest extent of a particular quality. For example, this hotel here is described as *the biggest on the island*, and this one is *the oldest in the resort*. These are **superlative adjectives**.

"You just need to read the descriptions and look for adjectives that match yours, or that mean the same thing. Remember, holiday companies won't keep using the same adjectives, because that would be boring. So, Izzy, you say you want a *lively* hotel. It's worth looking at hotels described as *bustling* and *buzzing* too, because those adjectives have a similar meaning. Sir Ralph, you could look for *quiet* and *restful* hotels too, because those adjectives have a similar meaning to *peaceful*."

Several hours later, Sir Ralph and Isabella found the perfect place.

**CYRENE HOTEL**

The hotel is tucked away in the quiet, old part of town, yet offers a disco in the evening and a heated pool with waterslides and a wave machine. Close to the shopping district and historic castle walls, the hotel stands in peaceful gardens containing the remains of a Roman villa.

*I suppose it's another two weeks at the dog kennel for me.*

"Well done!" said Max. "I suppose you want me to go and book it now?"

"Yes, please," said Isabella and Sir Ralph, at the same time.

*Top Tips!*

Pick your adjectives carefully. Some are more powerful than others, so avoid boring ones like *nice* or *good*. Think of better ones with a similar meaning and be careful not to use the same word twice!

## Did you know?

Adjectives work really well with **adverbs**.
*The dog barked.*
This sentence doesn't say very much. Adjectives and adverbs could change it to:
*The little dog barked happily* or *the fierce dog barked ferociously.*

# Cracking the Code

One afternoon, Isabella returned from school to find a note from Sir Ralph waiting for her. He was on the brink of a scientific breakthrough in his study of wood sap. During his research, he had chopped up most of the furniture in the house, including Spotless' kennel, so Isabella really hoped this message would contain good news.

The trouble was that when Sir Ralph was excited, although he could write faster than anyone she knew, he completely forgot about **punctuation**, so his messages never made any sense.

> hello izzy it's dad wow it's been an exciting day i have been to see spotty perkins did i ever tell you about him anyway i needed to ask him about types of tree sap the african pine canadian spruce and spanish oak and it looks like i was right all along see you later dad

*I wish they'd invent some software to deal with all this punctuation!*

"OK, Spotless, let's try to work out what Dad is on about. First of all, I need to break it up into **sentences**. Sentences are complete chunks of writing that make sense on their own. Each one will need a capital letter at the start, and a **full stop**, **question mark**, or **exclamation mark** at the end. Most sentences need a full stop, but questions end with a question mark and sentences that describe a surprise or deliver an order can end with an exclamation mark.

"There are some **proper nouns** in there and they need to start with capital letters too, as does the word *I*, which is always a capital letter.

"Then we can use **commas** to break some of the sentences up into manageable chunks. Commas can separate **clauses** in a sentence, go between items in a list, or signal where your reader needs to pause. Sometimes you can use **brackets** to make sentences easier to read, too. They go round extra bits of information, so if you take the brackets and the information they contain away, the sentence still makes sense. Now, let's see if we can work this out."

Hello, Izzy, it's Dad. Wow! It's been an exciting day. I have been to see Spotty Perkins. Did I ever tell you about him? Anyway, I needed to ask him about types of tree sap (the African Pine, Canadian Spruce and Spanish Oak) and it looks like I was right all along. See you later,

Dad.

"Brilliant!" exclaimed Isabella. "It looks like Dad's finished his research, so the rest of the furniture is safe, for now at least!"

*Top Tips!*

Use exclamation marks sparingly, or they lose their impact. Save them for really dramatic points in your writing.

## Did you know?

In 1802, American author Timothy Dexter published his book *A Pickle for the Knowing Ones*, without a single punctuation mark. It was so hard to read that people complained, so he added pages full of various punctuation marks at the end, and told his readers to "pepper and salt it as they please"!

# He Said What?

"I simply don't believe it!" Max threw down his newspaper in disgust. He had been reading a report about Brian Rocke, the manager of his favourite football club.

"Listen to this, Izzy – 'After yesterday's defeat at the hands of New Town, Brian Rocke says he will reconsider his position at the club.'"

"Oh, Max, I wouldn't believe anything you read in *The Daily Buzz*. They once said Dad's automatic nail clipping machine was the most important invention since sliced bread and we all know what happened to that."

"Yes, Izzy. My feet will never be quite the same again," laughed Max.

"Exactly. *The Daily Buzz* haven't even used Mr Rocke's own words. What they've printed is **reported speech**, and that's only as reliable as the person doing the reporting.

"Why don't you have a look in *The Monitor*? They take a lot more trouble with their reports, so you're much more likely to get the truth. They've covered the match too, but they've used **direct speech**. That means that if the journalist is being honest, those should be the actual words that Mr Rocke used."

"Fantastic news, Izzy. But how did you know that was direct speech?"

"Well, look at the first report. The reported speech has the same **punctuation** as a normal **sentence**: **commas**, **full stops**, that sort of thing. But the second reporter has put Mr Rocke's quote inside **speech marks**, so you know that those are his actual words. She has started off by explaining that it's him who is talking, then she's put a comma and then the speech marks. At the end of the sentence, she's put a full stop inside the speech marks."

After the match Brian Rocke explained, "I'll stay put for as long as I have the support of the players and fans. When they tell me to go, I'll reconsider my position at the club. But not a moment before."

*Say what you like about The Daily Buzz; they know a great invention when they see one!*

"I see. So is direct speech always better than reported speech?" asked Max.

"No, they are both useful," explained Isabella. "Direct speech often seems more believable and it's useful if two characters in a story are talking to each other. However, reported speech is useful if you want to include what someone says in your story, without him or her actually being in the story at that point."

"I see, and following the rules about punctuating speech makes sure your readers know whether they are reading direct or reported speech, right?"

"Spot on, Max. Using your common sense when you choose a paper can save you from reading rubbish about your team too!" laughed Isabella.

## Top Tips

With direct speech, you can say who is speaking before or after their quote. Don't keep using the word *said* though. Try using more powerful alternatives, like *exclaimed*, *demanded*, or *joked*, depending on *how* your character is talking.

## Did you know?

You should start a new line each time a different character starts talking, to make it easier for your reader to work out who is saying what to whom.

# Short Cuts

Isabella was sitting at the table, working her way through a pile of homework. She was supposed to be going ice-skating with friends later, but at this rate she'd be there all day.

"I'd better text Sophie and tell her I can't make it. I wish you could invent something to make writing quicker, Dad. If I could do my homework as fast as I can text, I'd be finished in no time."

"Well, I can't do that, but there is a way you can save a bit of time and effort when you're writing. You can sometimes join two words together, by taking out one or more of the letters and putting an **apostrophe** in their place. This is called **contraction** and it works with things like *I am*, which becomes *I'm*, *we are*, which becomes *we're*, and *did not*, which becomes *didn't*. Most of the time it's straightforward, but there are a couple of tricky ones to watch out for. Look, I'll make a list for you."

Izzy's list of timesaving contractions

| | |
|---|---|
| he is | he's |
| she is | she's |
| we will | we'll |
| you are | you're |
| they are | they're |
| we have | we've |
| would not | wouldn't |
| could have | could've |
| cannot | can't |
| it is | it's |

Take care with

| | |
|---|---|
| will not | won't |
| shall not | shan't |

*Cutting corners without breaking the rules, eh? I wonder if that would work with the dusting ...*

18

"What else are apostrophes used for, Dad?"

"Well, you use them when you want to say that something belongs to someone. *Izzy's huge pile of homework*, for example."

"Very funny, Dad. So you just add an apostrophe, then *s*?"

"You do for **singular** or **collective nouns**, unless they end in *s*. So you would write *the boy's football* and *the children's playground*."

"And if they end in *s*?"

"Ah, good question. **Plural** or singular nouns that end in *s* just have the apostrophe added to the end. So with those you would write *Spotless' bone*, or *the girls' books*."

"Brilliant, Dad. Anything else I need to know about using apostrophes like that?"

"Yes, Izzy. It's important to remember that **pronouns** usually don't have an apostrophe. So *its, his, hers* or *theirs* don't have apostrophes. The only exception is *one's*, but the pronoun *one* isn't used very much now anyway."

"So that should save you some time, eh? Get your skates on and you'll be finished in no time. Get your skates on, get it?"

"Yes, Dad," groaned Isabella. "I'm afraid I do."

### Top Tips!

Take care with *it's* and *its*. Remember, *it's* is short for *it is*. The apostrophe is there to show that the second *i* is missing. If you want to say that something belongs to *it*, you need the pronoun *its*, which never has an apostrophe.

## Did you know?

Contraction is great for direct speech and for informal writing, like writing a letter to a friend. For more formal writing, the longer version is usually better.

# A Crabby Connection

Isabella found some of her old school books from when she was very little. "Oh look, Dad! Look at the little pictures I drew; and my stories! They seem so babyish now."

"That's because young children tend to write in very short **sentences**, using maybe just one or two **clauses**."

"What's a clause, Dad?" asked Isabella.

"A clause is a group of words that make sense together. **Simple sentences**, like the ones in your old stories, just have one clause.

*I can kick a ball.*

"However, using two or more clauses in a sentence lets you link ideas together, like this sentence here.

*I can kick a ball and I can run fast too.*

"That is called a **compound sentence**. It links the ball with the running, and both clauses have equal weight. **Complex sentences** are even harder to write, but can flow better when you read them. In a complex sentence, one clause is often called the **main clause**. It makes sense on its own and contains the most important information. Take the sentence *I used to play football, in the park. I used to play football* is the main clause. The rest of the sentence is called the **subordinate clause**, because it just adds to the main clause and wouldn't make sense on its own."

IZZY'S BOOK

binoculars

photograph

Did someone say claws? Take a look at these!

"So what about the sentence *I used to play football, in the park, when I was younger*? Which is the main clause and which is the subordinate clause?" asked Isabella.

"Sometimes a clause is **embedded** in a sentence. In that sentence, the clause *in the park* is embedded in the main sentence. If you took it away, the rest of the sentence would still make sense."

"Using lots of clauses in your sentences must become very complicated," worried Isabella.

"True, and simple sentences can be great for making an impact with an important piece of information, but too many of them make your writing hard to read. Clever use of clauses helps your reader to make the connection between different ideas and makes your writing flow."

## Top Tips

Complex sentences can make your writing flow much better, but if they get too long and complicated they can be hard to read. Unless you are confident you can make it work, it's safest to stick to two or three short clauses.

## Did you know?

**Commas** can be useful to separate clauses, or you can use words like *because, when, unless* or *if*, to link two clauses together. Words like these are called **conjunctions**.

# One Slice at a Time

*I hope the birthday boy gets the biggest slice!*

It was Max's birthday so he had a night off from cooking and ordered pizza for the family instead.

When it arrived, Spotless was all set to guzzle the whole thing, without even waiting for it to be cut into slices.

"Steady on, boy," said Max. "Only a quarter of that is for you; the rest is for us. If you ate the whole thing you'd be sick."

Sir Ralph looked up from a book he was reading. "Yes, a bit like trying to read a whole page of this book without any breaks."

"What do you mean, Dad?" frowned Isabella.

"Well, just like a pizza needs to be cut up into slices, a piece of writing needs to be broken up into **paragraphs**. Paragraphs are the sections in a piece of writing. Each section should have a different flavour. A new paragraph might mean a new topic, a change of time or place in a story, or show that a new character is doing something or speaking.

"Sometimes, in short stories, you can simply start new paragraphs for the beginning, the middle and the end. However you slice it up though, using paragraphs should help you to organise what you want to say, so you need to think about them when you're writing your plan."

"Paragraphs also make it easier for readers to follow what you are trying to say," Max added. "Leaving a line between paragraphs shows your reader that you are about to start a new part of the story, or write about a slightly different topic. It also makes the whole page look less daunting. Some people **indent** the first line of a new paragraph too, to make it even clearer."

"Just like slicing up this pizza will make it easier to eat. Come on – let's get on with it before it gets cold!" said Isabella.

*Top Tips!*

If it looks like a paragraph is getting too long, start a new one. The person marking your paper will be put off by great long chunks of writing.

## Did you know?

**Non-fiction** writing doesn't necessarily have to be written just in paragraphs. You may be able to present some of the information as bullet points, but you should always start off with an introductory paragraph.

# Lost and Found

The Witherbottoms woke up one morning to discover that Spotless' basket hadn't been slept in. A search of the garden revealed a hole by the fence, just big enough for Spotless to squeeze through.

Sir Ralph was distraught. "Oh, Izzy, he's gone. He was such a sweet puppy, such a good dog."

"Sir Ralph, calm down," said Max. "You're talking about him in the **past tense**, as if he's dead. Wherever he is, I'm sure he's just fine. Let's write some posters to put up around town, and we'll use *all* the **tenses**, OK?"

"Good idea," said Isabella, "but what are tenses?"

"Tenses tell us *when* something happened. The past tense lets us talk about things that have already happened. To write in the past tense, you need to change the **verb**. Most past tense verbs end *ed*, although you sometimes have to change the spelling of the verb a bit before you add the *ed*. However, some verbs change completely in the past tense, and those are called **irregular verbs**. Let's write out a list of some of them."

"OK, Dad," said Isabella. "We can use some of those to tell people how Spotless escaped. How about,

*Our dog Spotless ran away last night. He crept under the fence into George Street."*

"Perfect," agreed Sir Ralph. "Now let's use the **present tense** to describe what he looks like. The present tense is used for talking about what's happening or how things are *now*. So we'll say, *Spotless is a tubby dog, with short sandy fur and no spots. He has floppy ears.*"

| Some irregular verb endings | |
| --- | --- |
| **Present tense** | **Past tense** |
| | went |
| go | brought |
| bring | ran |
| run | swam |
| swim | crept |
| creep | told |
| tell | was |
| am | thought |
| think | |

"What about the **future tense**, Dad? How can we use that for our poster?"

"Well, the future tense talks about things that will happen, or might happen. The verb is the same as the present tense, but you have to use another verb, like *will*, *shall* or *might*, as well. Let's say that we will give a reward to anyone who brings back Spotless."

> What does the future hold for poor Spotless?

**LOST**

Our dog Spotless ran away last night. He crept under the fence into George Street.

Spotless is a tubby dog, with short sandy fur and no spots. He has floppy ears.

There will be a reward for anyone who brings him back.

"Good," said Izzy. "I'll grab my coat and shoes and go out to put up the posters. Don't worry, Dad. I'm sure we'll find old Spotless in no time."

As Izzy went into the hall, she heard a faint sound of snoring and caught a glimpse of a tail sticking out from underneath her coat.

"Oh, Spotless!" she growled.

Top Tips

Time words or phrases are useful for telling your reader exactly when something happened. Try using words or **phrases** like *last week*, *at the moment*, or *next year*. They will also help to remind you which tense you should be using.

## Did you know?

Most stories are told in the past tense, but with practice you can move around in time within your story, using flashbacks or a mini-story within the main story. You could even write about what your character thinks might happen in the future. Just be careful not to slip from tense to tense by mistake.

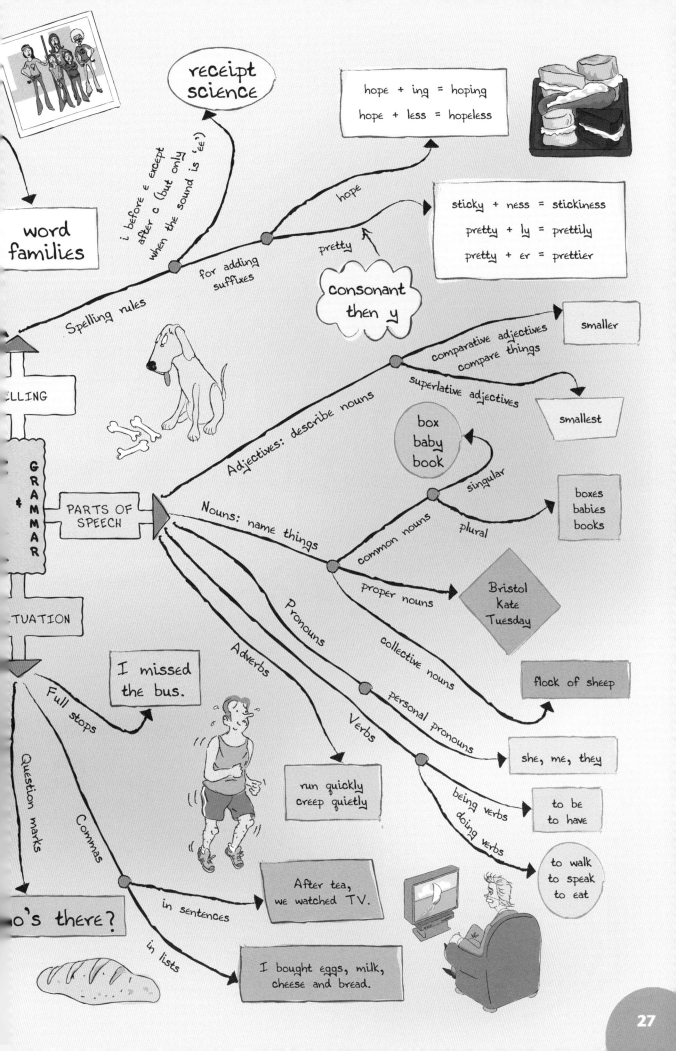

receipt
science

hope + ing = hoping
hope + less = hopeless

word
families

i before e except
after c (but only
when the sound is 'ee')

Spelling rules

for adding
suffixes

hope

pretty

sticky + ness = stickiness
pretty + ly = prettily
pretty + er = prettier

consonant
then y

comparative adjectives
compare things

smaller

superlative adjectives

smallest

Adjectives: describe nouns

box
baby
book

singular

boxes
babies
books

GRAMMAR

PARTS OF
SPEECH

Nouns: name things

common nouns

plural

proper nouns

Bristol
Kate
Tuesday

SPELLING

PUNCTUATION

Pronouns

collective nouns

flock of sheep

Adverbs

personal pronouns

Full stops

I missed
the bus.

Verbs

she, me, they

run quickly
creep quietly

being verbs

to be
to have

doing verbs

Question marks

Commas

to walk
to speak
to eat

Who's there?

in sentences

After tea,
we watched TV.

in lists

I bought eggs, milk,
cheese and bread.

# Revise Time

**1** Find the correctly-spelt word from each pair in the wordsearch grid.

a shamefull or shameful?

b skiing or sking?

c hungrily or hungryly?

d tryed or tried?

e dared or dareed?

f rakeing or raking?

g gracful or graceful?

h lovly or lovely?

| h | u | p | g | a | e | v | w | k | h |
|---|---|---|---|---|---|---|---|---|---|
| l | o | v | i | d | e | r | v | s | u |
| e | w | g | r | a | d | d | w | l | n |
| m | o | h | g | r | a | k | i | n | g |
| r | e | q | s | e | l | n | d | e | r |
| t | r | i | e | d | p | k | l | e | i |
| i | r | s | h | a | m | e | f | u | l |
| y | h | k | t | c | k | w | e | l | y |
| b | r | i | w | q | a | l | f | y | o |
| u | t | i | t | e | w | d | l | j | p |
| f | t | n | r | a | d | e | h | i | l |
| w | s | g | r | a | c | e | f | u | l |
| l | o | v | e | l | y | i | i | n | d |
| h | r | y | l | f | e | b | s | w | q |

**2** Add the punctuation to this passage. The capital letters are in the right places to get you started, but don't forget the apostrophes!

Jack came into the room Hello Ben he said Are you nearly finished Ben looked up from his homework Its pretty difficult but Im nearly there Great exclaimed Jack Then we can play football

**3** Megan chose this outfit to wear to the cinema last night. Using the past tense, write a description of the outfit, choosing suitable adjectives, pronouns and nouns from the box, or using your own.

| **Adjectives** | green | frilly | short | spotty |
|---|---|---|---|---|
| **Pronouns** | she | he | they | we |
| **Nouns** | hat | trousers | skirt | trainers |

_____

_____

_____

**4** Rewrite these pairs of simple sentences as longer, complex sentences. You don't have to use all the words.

a   My bag was blue. I left it on the bus.

_____

_____

b   I went swimming. I went after tea.

_____

_____

c   I went to Spain. I went for my holiday.

_____

_____

**5** Read these statements about paragraphs and write 'T' for true or 'F' for false in the boxes.

a   Stories should only have two paragraphs. ☐

b   Paragraphs can help you organise what you want to say. ☐

c   You should leave a blank line between paragraphs. ☐

d   Paragraphs are always one sentence long. ☐

e   A new paragraph is a sign for your readers that you have changed topic, or are writing about a different time or place in a story. ☐

f   It's a good idea to start thinking about paragraphs when you are planning your story. ☐

# Hunting High and Low

Sir Ralph was packing for a trip and sent Isabella down into the cellar to find his suitcase.

"You're joking, Dad. It's a terrible mess down there. How am I supposed to find your case amongst all that junk?"

Sir Ralph laughed. "Looking for stuff down there is like searching for information in a piece of text. You can either **skim** through, to get a *general* idea of what the piece of writing is about. Or you can **scan**, which means looking for a *specific* piece of information. In other words, you can either have a quick look to see what sort of junk you're up against, or you could sort through it systematically, looking for the suitcase."

Isabella piped up. "At school, we often have to locate bits of information in **fiction** and **non-fiction** texts, so that we can answer questions in tests. The trick is to read the question really carefully, to find out whether you need to skim for general meaning, or scan for a specific fact. Either way, it's a good idea to read the whole piece through carefully, in case there's a better answer further down.

"Our teacher says that it's really easy to pick up marks in tests for this kind of question, but it's easy to make mistakes if you rush them. If the question is asking you to retrieve a piece of information, you should never put down your own thoughts

*I'll do it! My ancestors were retrievers you know!*

and ideas, just the information from the text. You can tell how much to write by the space that has been left for you on the paper. Sometimes you just have to pick one answer from a selection. That's called a multiple-choice question. Other times you might just need one or two words, or a whole **sentence**."

Sir Ralph clapped his hands. "Very good, Izzy. You shouldn't have any trouble finding my suitcase with searching skills like that!"

### Top Tips!

After some questions on the reading paper, there will be a pair of **brackets** with a page reference, showing you where to find the information.

## Did you know?

We can skim quite quickly through a piece of text because we recognise the shape of common words, without actually having to read them. The more we read, the more quickly we can skim – so keep reading!

# Story Detective

When Max went into the library of the Witherbottom house one afternoon, he found Isabella scowling angrily in a corner.

"Whatever is the matter, Izzy?" he asked.

"Look Max, I've got this text to read and some questions to answer, but the answers aren't in the text. I've read it three times and they are definitely not there," Isabella complained.

Max read the questions carefully. "Calm down, Izzy. You just need to be a bit of a detective. These questions are asking you to use **inference and deduction** to find the answers. That means you have to look for *clues* in the text and *imagine* what the characters are feeling to come up with the answers. Let's read through the story and see what we can find out."

> The dark castle stood brooding against the skyline. Mina shivered, in spite of the warm sunshine, and looked at Sam. He seemed so calm; she couldn't let on how afraid she felt.
>
> As they approached the castle the walls rose threateningly above them, blocking out the blue sky and soft white clouds, which scudded cheerfully past.
>
> With a last look over their shoulders, the pair left the safety of the hillside and walked uncertainly through the gates.

"Right, Max, the first question asks why you think Mina won't tell Sam she is afraid. I think she can see that he isn't afraid and she doesn't want him to think she is a coward," suggested Isabella.

"Well done, Izzy!" said Max. "Let's try the next one."

"The second question asks why I think the author used the word *threateningly* to describe the castle walls," said Isabella. "I think that word suggests that something about the castle is dangerous and that the children aren't safe there. It builds up

So that's what they call reading between the lines!

suspense and makes me think that something scary is going to happen later in the story."

"Good work, Izzy. Now, the last one asks why you think Mina and Sam look back before they go inside the castle. What do you think?"

"OK. Well, if I was going into a dark, scary castle, I wouldn't be sure if it was a good idea," pondered Isabella. "I think they are having second thoughts about leaving the safety of the outside world behind them, because they don't know what they'll find inside."

"Great! You see, these questions are easy, if you take your time and imagine how the characters are feeling," explained Max. "Top detective work, Izzy!"

## Top Tips!

When you write down your answers, take great care to say exactly what you mean. The examiner can't read your mind and you won't get marks for details you miss out.

## Did you know?

We use inference and deduction all the time when we're reading. If stories always told us exactly how things and people looked, acted and felt, they would be extremely long, and very boring!

# Precious Preparations

*How about preparing me a snack?*

Max was packing a bag for Sir Ralph, who was going away for a week. "It's best to be prepared for anything," he said to Isabella, folding up a woolly jumper and a thin shirt.

"I could do with getting prepared too," replied Isabella. "I've got a reading test at school tomorrow and I'm really nervous, because I don't know what to expect."

"I think I can help you there. My friend Jenkins is the butler at number 42 and the boy there did his reading paper last year. Jenkins helped him prepare and told me all about it.

"You'll be given a Reading Booklet, which will contain a mixture of **fiction** or poems and **non-fiction**, all based on a theme," explained Max. "You have to read the texts carefully, then answer the questions in the answer book."

"OK, so what do I have to remember about reading fiction?" asked Isabella.

"Well, the first thing to remember is that fictional stories tend to use more creative techniques like **simile** and **metaphor**, and the author may well use images to suggest how characters are feeling. So you need to use your skills in **inference and deduction** to understand the story properly.

"Start by reading the text on the question paper and make notes about things that you notice in the margin. It's helpful to underline the names of characters too. When you have read it all carefully, you're ready to answer the questions."

"What sort of questions will there be, Max?" asked Isabella.

"There are four basic types. The first is multiple-choice, where you just pick the best answer from a selection. They are usually worth one mark each. For example, you might be asked to pick out what one of the characters said.

"The second type is a one-word or short phrase answer. You might have to retrieve a piece of information, or use simple inference. So the question might give you a **sentence** from the text that describes how a character feels and ask you why they feel that way.

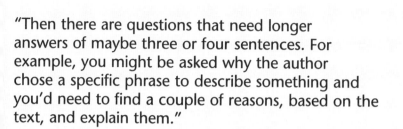

"Then there are questions that need longer answers of maybe three or four sentences. For example, you might be asked why the author chose a specific phrase to describe something and you'd need to find a couple of reasons, based on the text, and explain them."

"And the final type?" asked Isabella.

"They are the three-mark answers, where you have to explain your answer fully, and find evidence from the text to back it up. You might have to say how you know that a character is feeling afraid. You would need to find phrases in the text that tell you and explain how the language builds up the feeling.

"Remember, though, even if you don't think you can write a three-mark answer, what you have written down might still be worth a mark or two. Look at the marks available and the space left for your answer, to help you decide how much to write."

Isabella sighed.

"Don't worry, Izzy," soothed Max. "Now you're prepared, you'll be fine!"

## Top Tips

If you come across an unfamiliar word, look at the context to help you work out what it might mean. If you're still not sure, don't waste time. It might become clearer later on.

## Did you know?

The questions on the reading paper are designed to build your understanding of the text as you go, so answer them in order, if you can.

# Reading Rules

Isabella was worried because she had a reading test at school the next day and she knew she would have to answer questions on some **non-fiction** texts. The trouble was that there were so many different types of non-fiction text. She went to find Max to see if he could help.

"Max, do you remember you said your friend Jenkins helped the boy at his house to get ready for his reading test?" she asked. "I don't suppose he told you anything about reading non-fiction, did he?"

"You're in luck, Izzy," said Max, smiling. "As it happens, he did."

"Oh good! I just don't know what to expect. There are so many types of non-fiction."

"Don't panic. The title of the text may well give you some clues. For example, if it is a question, like *Who Invented Football?*, the text is probably a discussion or persuasive text. On the other hand, if it is called *How to Grow a Sunflower*, you can be pretty sure it is a list of instructions. The type of text used in the papers varies. It might be an interview, an advert, a letter or a report of some sort.

"Start by looking at the structure of the text. Does it have headings, bullet points or boxed information? If it does, how do they help the writer to organise the information? Make notes in the margin if you notice a special definition, or if the type of text changes, say from a chronological account to a list of bullet points. Then you can look at the questions in the answer book."

"What kinds of questions will there be?" asked Isabella.

"You'll get the same four types of question as you do for fiction texts: multiple-choice, short answer, longer answer and explanatory answer. There will be some one-mark information retrieval questions, and you may be asked questions about the purpose of the text, or the title chosen for it. All these questions will probably be worth one mark each.

"You might also be asked why the author used a word or phrase. For these questions, you will need to use **inference and deduction** again. Longer, two-mark questions might ask you to find and list

related pieces of information in the text, or maybe to give possible reasons why something in the text happened.

"Finally, three-mark questions need a longer explanation with evidence from the text. So a question might state an opinion and ask whether you agree with it, based on what you have read. You would need to make up your mind and find several pieces of evidence to back up your answer."

"Thanks, Max," said Isabella. "Sounds fairly straightforward, I suppose."

"Just take your time, Izzy," urged Max, "and if you finish with time to spare, read through your work carefully. Correcting mistakes at the end will earn you extra, precious marks."

Q. Spotless is:
a) dashing
b) heroic
c) handsome
d) All three!

## Top Tips!

The four main types of question mentioned above are the ones that appear most often, but you might also be asked to put some **sentences** into chronological order, or to link sets of related words.

## Did you know?

Each section in the answer book contains questions on a different text from the Reading Booklet. There may, however, be some questions at the end on all of the texts.

# Secrets in the Sand

Isabella was gazing at the newly-painted yellow walls of the kitchen.

"Yellow," she said. "I can only see yellow."

"That's because that wall you're staring at is yellow," replied Max. "What did you expect?"

"No, I don't mean the wall," explained Isabella. "I mean this stupid poem. I'm supposed to read it and answer some questions on it, but to me it's just all about yellow. What does it mean, Max?" asked a frustrated Isabella.

Sahara

Silence

Hazy trees tremble in parched awe

As brittle branches surrender.

Jewel-hued mirage

Green and blue and cool.

Distant deceiver of desperate eyes.

Soon be gone.

Yellow sands go on and on.

"Well, for starters, it's obviously about the desert," began Max. "The first verse talks about how hot and dry the trees are. They aren't really trembling, of course, but the poet thinks they look that way, probably because of heat haze. Describing *things* as if they were *people* is called **personification**. It's a good way of creating atmosphere, especially in a poem. The poet has used **alliteration** too, in the phrase *brittle branches*."

"OK, so we have lots of sand and dead trees, and nothing else," complained Isabella.

"Are you sure?" tested Max. Isabella looked confused, so he continued.

"Well, the next verse talks about a mirage. That's something people sometimes think they can see in a desert, but it's not really there. I think the poet is suggesting that someone is in the desert. Someone with *desperate eyes*. Perhaps someone stranded? I wonder if the phrase *Soon be gone* is talking about the mirage, or the person? Certainly the final line hints at a kind of hopeless desperation. Quite chilling, I think!"

*Phew! All this talk about heat has made me thirsty!*

"You're right, Max, but what about these questions? This one-mark question is asking for another example of personification. How about the mirage as *distant deceiver*?"

"Yes, that would be perfect," agreed Max. "Now, how about this two-mark question? It asks how colour is important in the poem. Now you can talk about all that yellow!"

"At last!" smiled Isabella. "Well, the poet describes a cool blue and green mirage. I like the way the colours are described as jewels. It makes them sound vivid and precious. The only colour that is really there though is the yellow sand, and that goes on and on. So the yellow becomes a symbol of being hopelessly stranded."

"Very good, Izzy. Ready for the three-mark question?" asked Max. "It asks what the poem makes you think the desert is like. How would you answer that?"

"Well, I'd want to talk about how hot and dry it is; so hot that it makes the trees brittle. I'd want to talk about the size of the desert, with sand going on for miles and miles. Finally, I'd say that it is cruel. There's no shade or water and it teases the stranded person with an image of an oasis that isn't real," finished Isabella.

"Excellent, Izzy!" said Max. "Now stop gazing at the wall and help me with this second coat of paint!"

## Top Tips!

Some questions about poetry will ask for the retrieval of facts and some will require **inference and deduction**, just like the questions about fiction.

## Did you know?

Most of the techniques for reading fiction work with poetry too. Just remember that although poems are usually shorter than stories, they are much more intense. Creative techniques like alliteration, **metaphor** and personification allow poets to cram a lot of meaning into just a few words.

what is it about?

setting

storyline

names

events

scan for specific facts

direct speech

skim for meaning

build up the word around the vowels

Information retrieval

multiple choice or very short answers

1 mark

2 or 3 line answers: simple inference or finding examples

2 marks

long, fully-explained answers about content or purpose of text

3 marks

Key facts

Test questions

Look for

READING NON-FICTION

boxed intro

bullet points

structure

headings

purpose of the text

Think about

choice of title

why the poet chose those words

choice of words

Think about

dark gloomy sinister

what does structure mean?

the title

alliteration

rhythm & rhyme

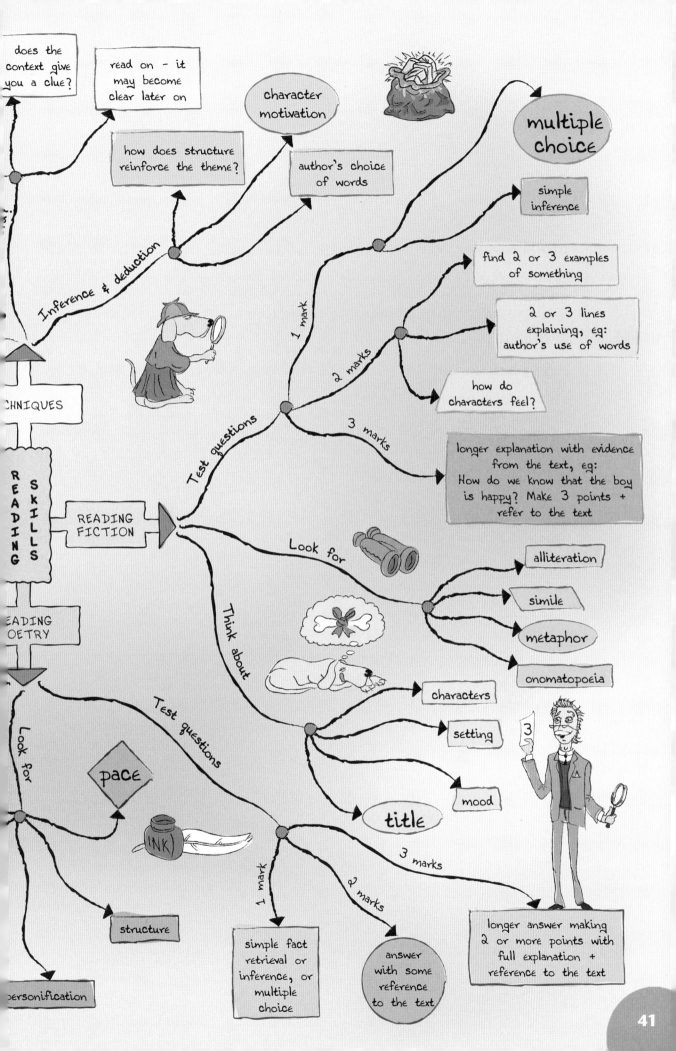

does the context give you a clue?

read on – it may become clear later on

character motivation

author's choice of words

how does structure reinforce the theme?

multiple choice

simple inference

find 2 or 3 examples of something

2 or 3 lines explaining, eg: author's use of words

how do characters feel?

1 mark

2 marks

3 marks

Inference & deduction

...CHNIQUES

longer explanation with evidence from the text, eg: How do we know that the boy is happy? Make 3 points + refer to the text

Test questions

READING SKILLS

READING FICTION

Look for

alliteration

simile

metaphor

onomatopoeia

Think about

characters

setting

mood

...EADING ...OETRY

Test questions

Look for

pace

title

INK

structure

1 mark

2 marks

3 marks

simple fact retrieval or inference, or multiple choice

answer with some reference to the text

longer answer making 2 or more points with full explanation + reference to the text

...ersonification

# Revise Time

This is an interview with famous film director Simon Sealberg about his latest hit film, *Buccaneers on the Bounty*.

### How would you describe *Buccaneers on the Bounty*?

Quite simply, it's a modern take on a classic story of swashbuckling pirates. We've taken the traditional tale of *Mutiny on the Bounty*, and brought it bang up to date to appeal to today's young audiences, with space-age technology and some female pirates for girls to relate to.

### Have you been surprised by the success of *Buccaneers on the Bounty*?

It has certainly gone down a storm, hasn't it! We had a fantastic cast and we knew the script was first class, so it would have been kind of disappointing if it hadn't been a success at the box office. But even we were surprised by how successful the computer-generated special effect sequences were and I'm sure they have played a big part in the success of the film.

### Any plans for a sequel?

There will be a sequel and we're already working on the script. I can't say too much about it at the moment, but I can promise you it will be well worth seeing!

## Read the interview and answer these questions.

1  **The film has female pirates:**

a  because it is space-age ☐

b  for girls in the audience to relate to ☐

c  because of the special effects ☐

d  because the script was first class ☐

2  **List three reasons why the film was so successful.**

_____

_____

_____

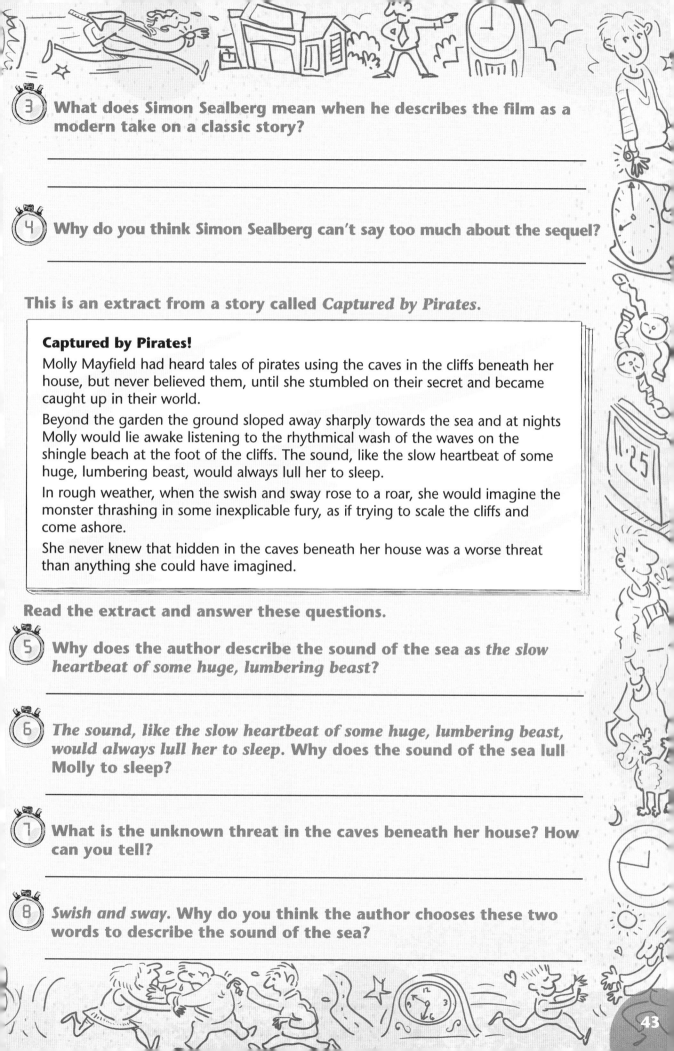

**3** What does Simon Sealberg mean when he describes the film as a modern take on a classic story?

_____

_____

**4** Why do you think Simon Sealberg can't say too much about the sequel?

_____

This is an extract from a story called _Captured by Pirates_.

**Captured by Pirates!**

Molly Mayfield had heard tales of pirates using the caves in the cliffs beneath her house, but never believed them, until she stumbled on their secret and became caught up in their world.

Beyond the garden the ground sloped away sharply towards the sea and at nights Molly would lie awake listening to the rhythmical wash of the waves on the shingle beach at the foot of the cliffs. The sound, like the slow heartbeat of some huge, lumbering beast, would always lull her to sleep.

In rough weather, when the swish and sway rose to a roar, she would imagine the monster thrashing in some inexplicable fury, as if trying to scale the cliffs and come ashore.

She never knew that hidden in the caves beneath her house was a worse threat than anything she could have imagined.

Read the extract and answer these questions.

**5** Why does the author describe the sound of the sea as _the slow heartbeat of some huge, lumbering beast_?

_____

**6** _The sound, like the slow heartbeat of some huge, lumbering beast, would always lull her to sleep._ Why does the sound of the sea lull Molly to sleep?

_____

**7** What is the unknown threat in the caves beneath her house? How can you tell?

_____

**8** _Swish and sway._ Why do you think the author chooses these two words to describe the sound of the sea?

_____

# Recipe for a Good Story

Sir Ralph rushed excitedly into the front room. "Guess what, Izzy. I had dinner with Arthur Steele last night. You know, the famous author. You'll never believe what I've got for you! You see, Mr Steele was talking last night about the secrets of writing a great story. He compared the perfect story structure to the delicious dinner we had last night – five different courses, each complementing the next – and he wrote it all down for you. Look!"

### Chez Louis

### Menu

### Starter
The big opening. Introduce your characters and setting. Grab that reader!

### Fish course
The build-up. Explain the events that lead up to the big dilemma in the story. Develop your characters as the events unfold.

### Main course
The dilemma. This is the problem that your characters have to solve; the heart of the story.

### Dessert
What happens next? How do your characters try to solve the problem they have found themselves with?

### Cheese and biscuits
Resolution. Is the problem resolved? If so, how? Or perhaps you want a cliffhanger ending, where your readers never find out what happens?

*That's what I call a story you can get your teeth into!*

"Wow, Dad. This is great!" said Isabella, "but I'm not sure I understand how this would work with a real story. I wish I could ask Mr Steele for an example."

"No need, Izzy," smiled Sir Ralph. "I took the liberty of asking him and jotted down what he said on my napkin. The story is from his latest thriller, and very gripping it sounds, too!"

**OPENING** Casey Crown has been released from prison and is met outside by his old bank-robbing partner Fingers Fitch.

**BUILD-UP** The pair plan a huge jewel robbery from an exhibition at the museum. They steal plans of the museum and work out how to switch off the alarms.

**THE DILEMMA** When they break into the museum they realise that extra security has been installed for the exhibition. They have just 60 seconds to cut through the glass, grab the jewels and make their escape, before the alarm goes off. Will they have time?

**THE EVENTS** The pair manage to steal the jewels but are not in time to escape before the alarm goes off and the automatic security shutters trap them in the museum. They hide behind an exhibit in the Egyptian gallery.

**THE RESOLUTION** The police arrive and search the museum. They find Casey Crown and Fingers Fitch but never recover the jewels, which are still hidden. The thieves plan to return for them once they have been released.

"Great, Dad, thanks!" said Isabella. "I wonder if Casey Crown and Fingers Fitch will ever get the jewels back. What a good story!"

"And all down to careful planning," said Sir Ralph. "Simple when you know how!"

## Top Tips

Your structure forms the basis of your story plan, so it is worth spending time getting it right. Don't worry – your plan does not get marked.

## Did you know?

In lots of short stories, each section of the structure is one **paragraph** long. Writing like this can help you to plan your story, but you do need to take care that your paragraphs don't become too long.

# Puzzled About Planning?

Sir Ralph was busy planning an expedition to Mexico. Being rather disorganised, he had asked Isabella to help.

"You need to plan things better, Dad. Planning something is like putting a jigsaw puzzle together. You have to make sure all the bits are there and then you do it step by step. Remember that story structure you brought back for me from your dinner with the author Arthur Steele? In a story plan, the structure is the first piece in the puzzle. Then you can add your characters and setting. The plan is also the time to write notes on any special ideas you have for words or **phrases** to use in your story."

"That's all very well for stories, Izzy, but I don't have time to waste making plans for this trip!" said Sir Ralph.

"Actually, Dad, our teacher says that making a good plan can *save* you time. She says that in a 45-minute writing test, you should spend the first ten minutes planning, or five minutes for a 20-minute test. Look at this story plan I did today."

### Opening
Kate and Mark go into town on the bus. It is raining hard.

### Build-up
They have a great time in town, then decide to go home.

### Dilemma
Kate loses her purse and bus ticket. Mark has no money for another ticket.

### Events
It's getting dark. Kate and Mark find a phone box to call home, but it isn't working. Then they see a policeman.

### Resolution
The policeman gives them a ride home. The next day he phones to say that Kate's purse has been handed in.

**Characters**
Kate: Ten years old, sensible. Long blonde hair, jeans, blue fleece, trainers.

Mark: Kate's younger brother, eight years old. Nervous. Jeans, trainers, blue coat, brown scruffy hair.

**Settings**
In town: Lots of bright lights reflected in the wet pavement. Hustle and bustle.

**Bus stop:**
Dark, cold, deserted. Wet and windy, broken street light.

**Special phrases:**
Mark had wild hair
Kate rummaged desperately
The dark crept around the children

"That's great, Izzy, but what if you make your plan and then have a better idea?" asked Sir Ralph.

"Then you use the better idea of course, as long as you can make it fit with what you have already written. Your plan is there as a guide, that's all. For example, if you found out that it would be snowing in Mexico, you'd take warm clothes with you, even if you hadn't put them on your original plan, wouldn't you?"

"Snow in Mexico? Ridiculous!" muttered Sir Ralph to himself. "Perhaps I'll pack my snowshoes anyway though, just in case."

> Sometimes I think Sir Ralph is one piece short of a jigsaw puzzle!

## Top Tips

Think of some really good phrases for describing people and places. You never know when you'll be able to use them in a story.

## Did you know?

Writing a good plan will save you time and help you to gain extra marks. Your plan itself won't be marked, although you may be asked to hand it in.

# Snack Attack

Isabella was busy making an enormous sandwich, piled high with all her favourite fillings.

"Steady on, Izzy," said Max. "How are you going to eat that? You know, it's not just the filling that counts. The bread is important too. My old school teacher was always telling us to think of a story as a sandwich, with the build-up, dilemma and events as the filling sandwiched between the opening and the resolution; the bread. He knew how important it is to get the bread right. After all, a story with a weak opening and resolution is no good at all."

"I see what you mean," replied Isabella. "So what makes a strong opening?"

"A strong opening sets the scene and often introduces the characters. It needs to be really gripping so your readers want to carry on reading. There are different ways to start your story. If you begin with a description of the setting, you need to choose really strong **adjectives** and **adverbs**, that paint a vivid picture for your reader. Think about the kind of story you are writing and how you want the reader to feel. If it is a spooky story and you want them to feel scared, you need to choose words that will create that mood.

"Or you could start with a description of your characters. It needs to be good, though, so your readers are interested in finding out what happens to them. You can even start with dialogue between your characters, but if you do, what they say has to be interesting enough to draw in your reader."

"You certainly know your stuff, Max. What makes a strong resolution, then?" asked Isabella.

"Ah, well they can be tricky, Izzy. You need to know how your story will end before you start writing really, so it doesn't just fizzle out. You could have a happy ending, or you could end with a moral lesson, like a fable. Either way, you need to bear it in mind as you write and be careful not to give the game away too early!"

"Or you might want a cliffhanger ending," Max continued, "where your characters are simply left in a dangerous or difficult situation, with no obvious way out. You need to be careful with those though – you can't just stop half way through!"

"I like those stories that have a sting in the tail," said Isabella. "You know, where you think it's going to end one way, but right at the end, something else happens."

"Yes, they're exciting," agreed Max. "They work particularly well in crime stories and thrillers. With any ending, though, you need to be planning it all the way along, to make it believable. Your story has to fit together into a tempting whole, a bit like your sandwich there. Any chance you could make one for me?"

Clearing out the fridge for a mega-sandwich? Same old story!

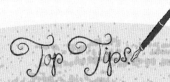

## Top Tips

Read as many stories as you can and look at how the author uses openings and endings.

## Did you know?

Cliffhangers are great for ending chapters in longer stories, or for episodes of things like soap operas. They make the reader, or viewer, want to come back for more.

# Blast from the Past

Isabella and Sir Ralph were looking through some old photographs, taken when Sir Ralph was at university.

"Oh, Dad, just look at those clothes," said Isabella. "And your hair! Your friends don't look much better either. Who's that, with the long skirt and those ridiculous collars on her blouse?"

"Ah, that's Rowena Muddleton," Sir Ralph reminisced. "Always cheerful and a quite brilliant chemist. She was a bit disorganised though. I remember once she mixed up the wrong chemicals and caused quite an explosion. Lives in the rain forest now, distilling chemicals from the plants there to use in medicines."

"Wow, she sounds like a character from a book," said Isabella. "I might use her in a story I'm writing. I could certainly write a great description of what she looks like based on that photo; and she sounds like she has a really interesting personality too. My teacher says that when you are writing about characters, you have to think about what kind of people they are, as well as what they look like. So you need to think about things like how they talk, where they live and how they get on with the other characters in the story. Thinking it all through at the start means that your characters will be more believable. Then you just have to choose really powerful **adjectives** to describe them. You can also use strong **verbs** and **adverbs** to talk about the things they do."

Crikey! Those clothes are like something from a horror story!

"Gosh, you do know a lot about characters, don't you, Izzy? Now, if you used Rowena in a story, you would need another character too. How about the other chap in the photo? He's called George Makin. Another gifted chemist, but rather hard to like. He was very unfriendly and had a dreadful habit of clicking his pen all day."

"I don't much like the sound of him!" said Isabella.

"Well, you know your readers don't have to like your characters, but they do need to be interested in what happens to them," explained Sir Ralph. "Sometimes nasty characters work really well, especially if they are punished in the end. Now how about making room for your old Dad in your story? I'm sure there would be space for one more character."

Isabella thought quickly. "Sorry, Dad. You see, you have to be careful not to include too many characters, otherwise you don't have space to describe them properly and they end up sounding really boring, and I wouldn't want to do that to you, Dad!"

## Top Tips!

When you are describing a character, stick to what is relevant to the story. There's no point saying that a character has a brother, for example, unless he plays a part in the story.

## Did you know?

Like Isabella, lots of writers base their characters on real people. They usually change their names and some of the details though, in case they recognise themselves!

# Picture Perfect

Isabella had decided to use two of her father's old university friends as characters in a story she was writing. Sir Ralph had described what they were like to her and she had an old photograph to help her write about what they looked like. Both characters were chemistry students, so Isabella wanted to use the chemistry lab as the setting for part of the story. The trouble was, she had no idea where to start, so she asked Sir Ralph.

"Well, Izzy, a good setting description includes what a place looks like, but also what it sounds and smells like," explained Sir Ralph. "I could tell you what time of day that photo was taken, and even what the weather was like. If you have all that information, you can paint a picture for your reader, so they feel like they're really there. Here's a checklist to help you remember what you need to find out about:

- What did it look like?
- What did it smell like?
- What did it sound like?
- What was the weather like?
- What time of day was it?

"So, to start with, the lab always looked rather a mess. There was usually lots of clutter about and lots of experiments going on. So there would be a lot of glass flasks and tubes, full of brightly coloured liquids. You would hear the hissing of the gas from the Bunsen burners, and bubbling and popping sounds from the experiments. There was usually quite a pong too, from all the chemicals. It smelt like rotten eggs.

"The photo was taken late one afternoon in January. I remember it was a terrible winter that year. Gusts of wind whistled eerily in the windows. The lab was bitterly cold most of the time, so we would warm our hands in the heat from the burners. Wonderful times!"

"Wow, Dad!" said Isabella. "The way you describe it really brings it to life. It's like I'm there. **Adjectives** like *bitterly cold* and *bubbling and popping sounds* help to paint a vivid picture, and using the **adverb** *eerily* to describe how the wind whistled in the windows is great, too."

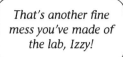

*That's another fine mess you've made of the lab, Izzy!*

"Glad I could help," smiled Sir Ralph. "Are you just having the one setting then?"

"No. I think some of the action will take place outside. Why?" asked Isabella.

"Well, moving from one setting to another is fine as long as you do it carefully," explained Sir Ralph. "Make sure your readers know you have changed setting, perhaps by starting a new **paragraph**, or using **connectives** like *meanwhile, back in the lab*, or *later that afternoon, in the park*… Also, try not to chop and change too much, Izzy, or your reader won't be able to keep up!"

"Great. Thanks for the tip, Dad. Now I'm off to get this story planned. See you later!"

## Top Tips!

When you are writing about your setting, think about how you want your readers to feel and choose adjectives that help to create that feeling. The same woodland setting could be dark and gloomy, or calm and peaceful. It's up to you!

## Did you know?

Most stories need strong characters and a great setting, but some stories are really about how the characters are feeling and the setting might not be that important. If you are sure that your story is one of these, spend less time on the setting and more on the characters.

# The Sorcerer's Apprentice

"Oh, this story just isn't working," snapped Isabella, who was trying to write something for her class tomorrow. "It's really boring."

Max overheard and took pity. "I tell you what," he said, "I'm no wizard, but I can teach you a few clever tricks that will bring any story to life. The secret to writing magical fiction is in the language you use.

"First of all, you need to pick really strong **adjectives** to describe your characters and settings. Then you throw in some great **verbs** and **adverbs** to describe what they do, and the other things that happen in your settings. If the first word that springs to mind is boring, or you've already used it, think of a **synonym** for it. Synonyms are words with similar meanings and there are usually plenty to choose from. So instead of *run* you could say *dash*, or you could replace *happy* with *ecstatic*. A **thesaurus** is a great place to find synonyms and you will probably be able to collect some good ones from your reading too.

"There are even cleverer tricks than these though. To start with, if you need to describe a sound, try using **onomatopoeia**. They are really effective words that sound like the noises they describe, like *whoosh, pop* or *clatter*.

"Then there is **alliteration**. That's where all the words in a **phrase** start with the same sound, like *Magic Max's marvellous miracles*. It's a good way to highlight an important phrase in a story or poem."

"These are great tips, Max! Have you got any more?" asked Isabella.

"How about **similes**? They help to paint a picture for your reader, by comparing one thing with another, using the word *as* or *like*. Things like *as quiet as a mouse* and *sleeping like a baby* are similes.

*Me? A pig? How dare he!*

"Or you could use a **metaphor**. That's where you write about something as if it really was something else, rather than just being *like* something else. So you might very well say *Spotless is a pig at mealtimes*.

"The real magic about all of these tricks is that you could use them in your stories and poems. You might even find a use for them in some types of **non-fiction** writing too."

"Amazing, Max!" gawped Isabella. "You're quite a conjurer when it comes to words, aren't you?"

Top Tips!

Don't save these tricks just for fiction writing. They can work wonders when you are writing advertisements and newspaper reports too.

## Did you know?

Lots of poems contain alliteration, and some have nothing else. They are a lot of fun, but tricky to read out loud!

*Peter Piper picked a peck of pickled pepper.*
*If Peter Piper picked a peck of pickled pepper,*
*Where's the peck of pickled pepper, Peter Piper picked?*

# Tricks of the Trade

Sir Ralph walked into the front room to find Isabella sitting on the sofa, book in hand, looking decidedly grumpy.

"Something the matter, my dear?" he asked.

"This story is just so much more interesting than the one I'm writing for school. I wish I knew the writer's secret."

"Maybe I can help you there, Izzy. You see, even the very best storyline and most beautifully described characters can still do with a bit of help sometimes. I find that asking a question in the story helps. Suppose your story was about a pair of friends who find a bag full of money in a park. You could write – *Would the friends be honest and hand it in to the police?* Readers love that kind of thing, because they can't wait to find out the answer to the question.

"Another good technique is to leave clues in the story about what might happen later. So one of your characters could say – *We should get away from here. What if the person this belongs to comes back?*

"Once your readers think that might happen, they will want to read on to find out. You do need to be quite subtle with these though, or you can end up giving too much away. Let your readers think it might happen, but keep them guessing!"

"Great, Dad. Have you got any other tips I could use?" asked Isabella.

"Well, the way you write your **sentences** can help, too. One way is to start a sentence with a **subordinate clause**, to build up suspense. So you could write – *Opening the bag, Luke was amazed to see the glint of gold from inside.*

"In this sentence, *opening the bag* is the subordinate clause.

"You can also use very short, **simple sentences** for impact too. Simple sentences only have one **clause**, but used sparingly they can be very dramatic, like this – *The bag had vanished.*

"Another clever way to write gripping sentences is to use **passive verbs**. Normally **active verbs** are better, but because passive verbs concentrate on what has happened, rather than on who or what has done it, they can build up suspense.

*The bag was grabbed roughly from him.*

"In this sentence, *was grabbed* is a passive verb. This makes the sentence scary, because it doesn't say *who* grabbed the bag.

"All of these subtle tricks can pull your readers in and make them want to read more. Clever, eh?" boasted Sir Ralph.

"These are great ideas, Dad. Maybe now I can make my story as appealing as the one I'm reading!" said Isabella, rushing off to her room.

*Not as appealing as this bone!*

These tricks get easier with practice, so try them out before you get into your writing test.

## Did you know?

Experienced authors sometimes leave false clues in their stories as 'red herrings', to confuse their readers.

# All Dressed Up

Isabella and Max were organising a surprise fancy dress birthday party for Sir Ralph. Isabella had already chosen a cowgirl outfit to wear and she was now going with Max to the fancy dress shop to choose a costume for Sir Ralph.

An hour later, after Max had tried on several outfits, they were no closer to finding the right one.

"This is exhausting! Let's narrow down the search a bit. What kind of stories does your father enjoy reading?" asked Max.

"Well, I know he likes science fiction. And he enjoys historical stories too, especially from the time of Henry VIII."

"Brilliant, Izzy. Science fiction and historical fiction are both **genres** of fiction. Genre is just a fancy word for a type of story. Books from the same genre often share similar themes and settings. The characters and even the storylines might have a lot in common, too. Thinking about what genre your story belongs to can give you ideas to help you write it. Your readers will also spot which genre it belongs to, so they may expect certain things from the story.

"For example, you're going to the party as a cowgirl. If you were a character in a story, it would probably be a western. Westerns are usually set in the Wild West. The cowboys ride horses and shoot guns, and at the end of the story, the good guy usually wins. Knowing all that, someone reading a western would be very surprised if a conflict between two cowboys was all about who had the nicest hat!"

"I see what you mean!" giggled Isabella.

"Science fiction stories have things in common too," explained Max. "They are all about how developments in science and technology could affect our lives and are often set in the future. Because they are completely made up, you can be pretty creative with your characters. They don't even need to be human! Your settings can be pretty wacky too. You can even make up new words for things, but you do need to

remember that your readers have to believe that it *could* happen, so they want to keep reading."

"Brilliant, Max! Not sure Dad would look good as an alien though. What about this Henry VIII outfit?" asked Isabella.

"Ah, that's much more like it. Historical fiction can be harder to write, because you are often writing about things that actually happened, so your settings and characters have to be believable. It's no good having a Tudor character watching TV! You need to know something about the clothes people wore, the houses they lived in, the work they did and the food they ate. Real authors often spend months researching all the historical details to make their stories realistic."

"Luckily all we have to do is find the outfit," laughed Isabella.

*I'm going as the Hound of the Baskervilles. Grrr!*

*Top Tips*

Thinking about genre can give you some good ideas, but don't just copy another story. Be original!

## Did you know?
Some stories can belong to more than one genre; historical romance is an example of this.

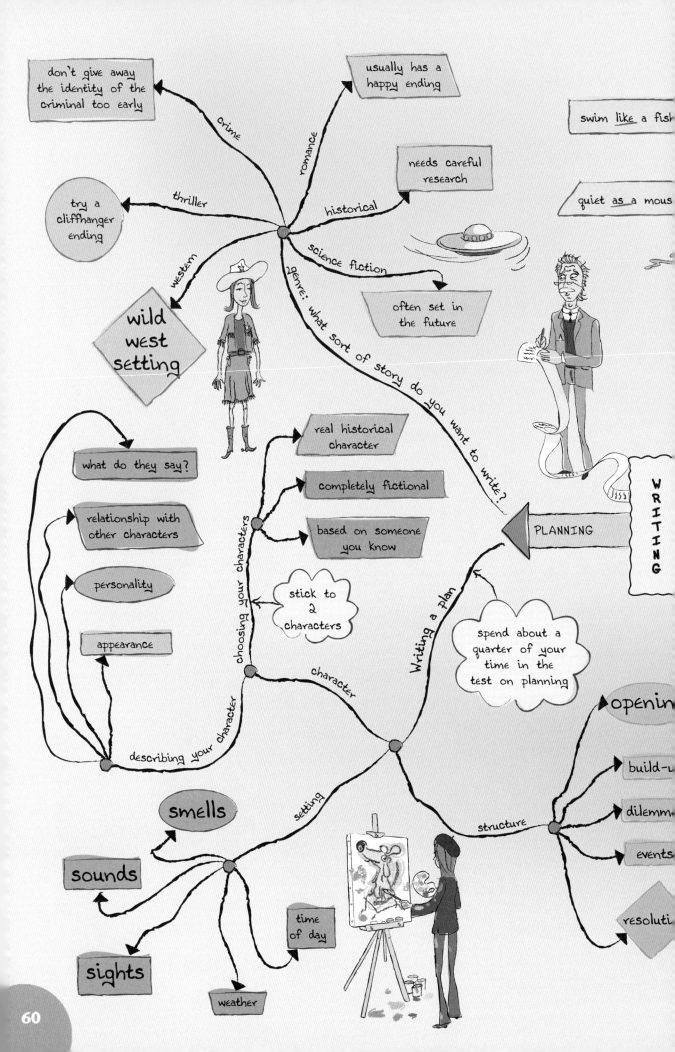

don't give away the identity of the criminal too early

usually has a happy ending

swim like a fish

try a cliffhanger ending

needs careful research

quiet as a mous

crime

romance

thriller

historical

science fiction

western

genre: what sort of story do you want to write?

wild west setting

often set in the future

PLANNING

WRITING

what do they say?

real historical character

completely fictional

relationship with other characters

based on someone you know

personality

choosing your characters

stick to 2 characters

Writing a plan

spend about a quarter of your time in the test on planning

openin

appearance

character

build-u

describing your character

dilemm

smells

setting

structure

events

sounds

sights

time of day

resoluti

weather

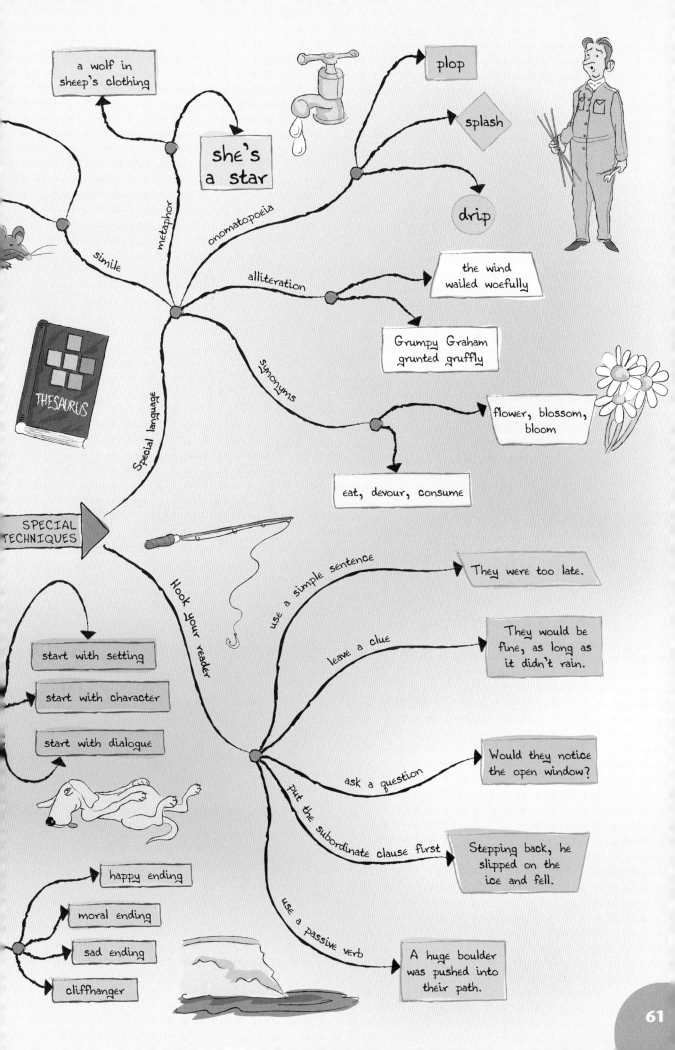

a wolf in sheep's clothing

she's a star

plop

splash

drip

metaphor

onomatopoeia

simile

alliteration

the wind wailed woefully

Grumpy Graham grunted gruffly

THESAURUS

synonyms

Special language

flower, blossom, bloom

eat, devour, consume

SPECIAL TECHNIQUES

Hook your reader

use a simple sentence

They were too late.

leave a clue

They would be fine, as long as it didn't rain.

start with setting

start with character

start with dialogue

ask a question

Would they notice the open window?

put the subordinate clause first

Stepping back, he slipped on the ice and fell.

happy ending

moral ending

sad ending

cliffhanger

use a passive verb

A huge boulder was pushed into their path.

**Look at this plan for a science fiction story, then answer the questions.**

### Opening

Rob and Lily live in 2662. The air has been poisoned so people live beneath huge glass domes. Rob and Lily are visiting the 'Beach Dome' for a holiday.

### Build-up

Rob and Lily find a small opening in the wall of their Dome. They decide to explore outside.

### Dilemma

Rob and Lily walk too far and cannot find the opening again to go back through. It begins to get dark.

### Events

The children are chased by a fierce Cybercat.

### Resolution

While they are running away, they come across the opening in the Dome. They climb through, but the opening is too small for the Cybercat to follow. They are safe.

**Characters**

Rob:

Lily:

**Setting**: Year 2662.

**Inside dome:** like a very beautiful garden, warm, bright

**Outside dome:** dark, cloudy, full of overgrown plants and strange animals

**Special language**

**1** Read the plan, then make up character notes for Rob and Lily.

_____

_____

_____

**2** Add four examples of special phrases you would use to describe the characters or settings.

_____

_____

_____

_____

**3** Using some of the techniques from pages 54–57, write an opening for the story, which includes a description of what it is like inside a dome.

_____

_____

_____

_____

**4** Using some of the techniques from pages 54–57, write an alternative cliffhanger ending for the story.

_____

_____

_____

_____

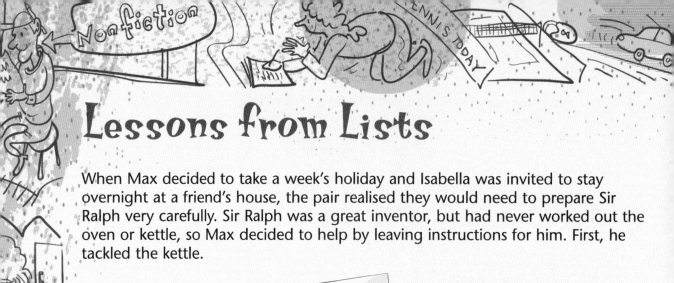

# Lessons from Lists

When Max decided to take a week's holiday and Isabella was invited to stay overnight at a friend's house, the pair realised they would need to prepare Sir Ralph very carefully. Sir Ralph was a great inventor, but had never worked out the oven or kettle, so Max decided to help by leaving instructions for him. First, he tackled the kettle.

Making a cup of tea

1. Boil kettle

2. Pour boiling water onto tea bag

3. Allow to brew for 2 minutes then remove tea bag

4. Add milk and sugar

"Sir Ralph, I've written you out some instructions for making a cup of tea. I've broken it down into clear, numbered steps, so you can be sure you are doing them in the right order.

"You should always use **imperative verbs** when writing instructions. They are verbs that give orders, like *boil* the kettle. I hoped you wouldn't think I was being rude!" checked Max.

"Good grief, no. To be honest though, Max, it's dinner I'm worried about. Whatever shall I eat?" asked Sir Ralph.

"I've left a recipe here for your favourite pancakes. Recipes are instructions too. The steps are numbered like before and there is a list of ingredients at the top, so you can check you have everything before you start. Recipes contain lots of specific information like weights and quantities of ingredients, so you need to be very careful to get those right."

## PANCAKES

### INGREDIENTS
100g plain flour
1 egg
250ml milk

1  Crack the egg into the flour
2  Add the milk and whisk to produce a smooth batter
3  Heat a lightly oiled frying pan
4  Pour a little batter into the pan
5  Cook until golden brown then turn and cook other side
6  Fill with chosen topping and roll up

What about instructions on Caring for Spotless?

"Great. Are instructions always numbered then, Max?" asked Sir Ralph.

"No, not always," explained Max. "If it doesn't matter what order the list is read in, you can use bullet points instead. Directions are yet another type of instructions. They describe a journey from start to finish, including the names of roads and landmarks along the way. You don't normally number directions or use bullet points, but it is really important to get the steps in the right order, or you'll get dreadfully lost!"

"I see. Now, have you left anything else for me?" asked Sir Ralph, hopefully.

"Just a take-away pizza menu, Sir Ralph, in case you can't manage the pancakes. I don't think even you need instructions for that!" laughed Max.

## Top Tips!

Make sure you always give your instructions a title, so your reader knows what the outcome will be.

## Did you know?

Instructions sometimes use **connectives** like *next*, *afterwards* and *then* to link the separate stages together.

# A Dog's Day

Spotless? I think Shameless would be a better name!

Isabella was thrilled when she won a writing competition in the local paper and was sent to report on the annual dog show. The trouble was that Spotless had been entered in the show and Isabella was sure he would misbehave.

Isabella was right to be worried. Spotless howled throughout the opening speech, chased his tail until the entire judging panel were so dizzy they had to sit down, leaped nimbly onto the Lady Mayoress' lap and devoured the silk flowers on her hat.

Not surprisingly, Isabella found it a hard story to write!

"Oh, Max, it was so embarrassing!" moaned Isabella. "I can't write about it!"

"Yes, you can," said Max, calmly. "Think of it as just another story. What would you normally do first?"

**What?**

**When?**

**Why?**

**Where?**

**Who?**

**How?**

"Well, there's a checklist of what you have to include; what happened, when and where, as well as how it happened, why, and who was involved," replied Isabella.

"You always put the key information first and work your way down to the less important facts. That's because newspaper editors cut stories from the bottom to make them fit the space on the page."

"Good, Izzy. What else do you need to think about, though?" encouraged Max.

Isabella thought for a moment. "Well, stories often include a quote from someone involved, to make it more interesting, so I suppose I could interview the Mayoress. The language you use is important too. Techniques like **alliteration**, **metaphor** and **simile** can all make a story more interesting. For example, I'm going to describe Spotless as a *disobedient dog* and say that he sprang onto her lap *like a wild animal*."

"Great! What else do you need? How about a headline?" asked Max.

"Yes. Headlines are important because that's what people read first to decide which stories they want to read," agreed Isabella. "They should be short and snappy and sum up the story."

"Well done, Izzy," said Max. "Now, why don't you have a go at writing it while I try and fix this hat? I couldn't get silk flowers so I had to get plastic grapes instead. Do you think she'll notice?"

# DOG SHOW CHAOS

The town's annual dog show ended in disaster on Thursday when one of the entrants broke its lead and attacked the Mayoress. The dog, named Spotless, sprang at the Mayoress like a wild animal, badly damaging an expensive hat.

Describing the disobedient dog, she said, "He didn't hurt me, he just wanted the flowers from my hat. He must have been hungry."

Sir Ralph Witherbottom, who owns Spotless, has apologised for the incident and says that his dog will not be entered in the rerun of the show, planned for next weekend.

## Top Tips!

When writing about an event, make sure your very first **sentence** sums up what the whole story is about.

## Did you know?

Newspaper reports should usually be objective – that means they don't take sides. They often have to put across two sides of an argument. There is more about writing a **balanced argument** later in the book.

# Party Planning

It was soon to be Isabella's birthday and Sir Ralph had told her that she could choose whatever sort of party she wanted. Max collected some leaflets for her to look at.

"Here we are, Izzy. What do you think of these?" he asked, showing her the leaflets. "You could have a swimming or trampolining party at the sports centre, go skiing at the dry-ski slope, or go for a meal at the new Mexican restaurant. What a choice!"

"Thanks, Max. The ski slope looks great, doesn't it? Listen to this. *'Picture yourself zipping down the newest and longest dry-ski slope in the country. Quite simply the most thrilling party solution in town! Party organiser skis free of charge!'*"

"That does sound good, Izzy. Whoever wrote that leaflet knows that the secret to selling something is to make it sound really exciting and good value for money. They have used lots of **superlative adjectives** like *newest*, *longest* and *most thrilling*, to persuade you that they can offer you the best party. They also know that good adverts inform as well as persuade. This leaflet has all the information you need as well, from opening hours and prices, to the address and phone number of the ski slope."

"This one isn't so good though. All the information is there, but it doesn't sound very exciting," said Isabella.

### PARTY WITH YOUR FRIENDS!

Parties of up to 15 people can swim or trampoline on a Saturday afternoon for £4 each.

Call in for more details.

"You're right, Izzy," agreed Max. "That leaflet isn't very interesting, is it? This one for the new Mexican restaurant has made a mistake too. It is full of superlatives and sounds fantastic, but there's no information at all about where it is, when it is open, or how much it would cost to have your party there."

# Nacho Heaven

Party at the brightest new restaurant in town! Enjoy authentic **MEXICAN** cuisine in **themed surroundings**.

Our **award-winning** chef uses only the freshest ingredients so you can be sure of **a delicious feast**.

*Ski slope? Think I'll slope out of that one…*

"I bet it's really expensive, then, or miles out of town so it would be hard to get to."

"Well, that's the problem with adverts that don't give you enough information. If you did want to book the restaurant for your party, there isn't even a phone number here to call for more information."

"The ski slope it is, then. I can't wait!" said Isabella, excitedly.

## Top Tips!

Leaflets are just one type of advertisement. Advertisments also appear on TV, on the radio and in magazines.

## Did you know?

The very first advertisement screened on ITV was broadcast in 1955, and advertised SR toothpaste. Even back then, advertisers knew the power of well-chosen **adjectives** and **similes**:

*It's tingling fresh.*
*It's fresh as ice.*
*It's Gibbs SR toothpaste, the tingling fresh toothpaste that does your gums good too.*

# Bright Sparks

Sir Ralph was close to making a breakthrough with his latest invention – everlasting light bulbs. He was trying to find a letter from an old friend that might just hold the answer, but his desk was in a terrible mess.

"Max!" yelled Sir Ralph. "I'm looking for a letter from my old pal Noah. Have you seen it?"

"Was it a formal letter, or an informal one?" asked Max.

"Is there a difference?" Sir Ralph asked back.

> Truglow Lamps and Fittings
> Hightown Industrial Estate
> Gwent
> GW4 9TN
>
> 5 January 2005
>
> Sir Ralph Witherbottom
> Long Lodge
> Newtown
> DV4 TNT
>
> Dear Sir Ralph,
>
> I am writing to request a further 35 of your everlasting light bulbs for product testing.
> The batch you sent last month all proved unstable at high temperatures and unless we can overcome this issue we will be unable to proceed to full-scale manufacture.
> Please send them at once.
>
> Yours sincerely
>
> Professor Witless

"Yes! Look, this letter from Truglow is formal. In formal letters, the address of the person writing the letter goes in the top right-hand corner, with the date below it. Further down, on the left, you put the address of the business you are writing to. Then you start your letter with the word *Dear*, and the person's name if you know it. If you don't, you use *Sir* for a man, or *Madam* for a woman.

"The first paragraph should say why you are writing, the next explains all the details and the last paragraph says what you want to happen next.

"If you know the name of the person you are writing to, you finish the letter *Yours sincerely*, and then sign your full name. If you used *Sir* or *Madam*, you finish it *Yours faithfully*."

"Gosh! I hope informal letters are a bit more straightforward," said Sir Ralph.

6 Mad March Court
Nether Wallop
Hants
NW14 8PQ
17 September 2003

Dear Ralph,.

Hope you are keeping well. Just wanted to let you know that I may have a solution to your light bulb problem. A friend of mine can make light bulb casings out of shatterproof glass!

Let me know if you are interested.

Take care old thing,

Noah

*Max is good at shedding some light on our problems!*

"Yes, they are. In an informal letter, you start with your address and the date, like before, but you don't need to put the address of the person you are writing to," explained Max.

"Then you just start your letter. It's polite to start by asking how the person is and you will need to start a new paragraph if you start writing about a different subject. Apart from that, the structure and the language are up to you.

"You can finish it however you like too. *Lots of love*, *Best wishes*, and *Take care* are all popular endings. Then you just sign your first name. Easy!"

"Max!" interrupted Sir Ralph. "This is the letter! Shatterproof glass is the solution to the problem. I must write to Truglow right away, and thanks to you, Max, now I know how to!"

## Top Tips!

Details matter when you are writing a letter. If you want to be taken seriously, watch out for your spelling and handwriting.

## Did you know?

People write fewer letters now that most of us use email and texts to stay in touch. Still, in this country alone, over 80 million letters and parcels are sent every day.

# The Cream Cake Caper

Isabella was just walking out of the bakery with some sticky buns for tea, when two men pushed past her, grabbed a tray of cakes and ran out again.

Back at the house, she enlisted Max's help to record what she had seen for the police.

"The police have asked me to write a **chronological report** of what happened. Any ideas how I do that, Max?" asked Isabella.

"Well, chronological reports, or **recounts**, as they are sometimes called, are quite simple. They record details about an event, so that someone who wasn't there can understand what happened. It's an information text, so your feelings and opinions don't come into it," explained Max.

"Because chronological reports are about things that have already happened, you use the **past tense**. You have to describe events in the order in which they happened, making sure you include all the important information. You use **connectives** like *first, afterwards* and *finally* to join the events together, so your readers can tell what happened first.

"The language you use is important too. You might need to use some technical language and you have to be very precise with the **adjectives** and **adverbs** you use to describe what people looked like and what they did. You also need to include information about things like which way they went and the time of day. However, don't use creative techniques like **alliteration**, **simile** or **metaphor**. In fact, the language in recounts should remain quite formal."

"Thanks, Max," exclaimed Isabella. "I'd better get cracking with this. The police are sure to catch the cake thieves soon. If they've scoffed all those cakes they won't be in any state to make their escape!"

I was in the Sticky Bun cake shop at about 10am on Tuesday, buying some cakes. After I paid, I turned to leave the shop but I was knocked sideways by two masked men.

One was tall and the other was short and fat. First, the men dashed behind the counter and grabbed a recipe book. After that, they shovelled cream slices into a sack, before making their escape.

The sack slowed them down and I was able to see that the tall man had grey hair and a tattoo of a chocolate éclair on his right hand. Both men scurried down Baker Street before turning into Friar's Square.

*I was there too. Give me a sticky bun and I'll tell you all about it!*

## Top Tips

Connectives are really important in recounts but don't use the same ones over and over again. *Then* is very boring, so only ever use it once!

## Did you know?

Chronological reports should be objective. They report things exactly as they happened, not how the writer felt about the events. Even so, recounts of the same event written by different people can be quite different, because people often have different perspectives

73

# A Dog's Life

Can't you let sleeping dogs lie?

Sir Ralph was surprised to walk into his study and find Isabella on her hands and knees, studying a sleeping Spotless intently.

"What on earth are you doing, Izzy?" he asked.

"I'm writing a non-chronological report for school about dogs and I thought Spotless might give me some inspiration. Maybe I should wake him up," pondered Isabella.

"Why don't you let your old Dad help instead? I was quite a whizz at writing reports when I was at school," boasted Sir Ralph.

Isabella looked dubious, but let him continue all the same.

"First of all, non-chronological reports are information texts. That means they describe the way things are, rather than trying to persuade the reader to take a particular point of view.

"Like most writing, you start with a plan. You need an introduction, which tells the reader what the report is about and what angle you are taking. So you would say your report is about owning a dog and perhaps make the point that it is hard work and needs careful thought.

"Then, rather than arranging the main information in time order, like a **chronological report**, you split it into topics, which go in any order. Once you have written about those, you finish with a conclusion, which draws all the points you have made together. So if you say that taking care of a dog is hard work, then you need to return to that in the conclusion as well."

"Sounds simple enough. Is there any special language I need to use?" asked Isabella.

"Yes, there is. Non-chronological reports are written in the **present tense**, using the impersonal voice. That just means that you would write *people love dogs*, rather than *I love dogs*. It's useful to use words that generalise too. So you could write *many dogs* are bought as puppies, or *all dogs* need lots of exercise. You will need technical words too, like *collar*, *puppy* and *immunisations*."

"Thanks, Dad. Anything else?" asked Isabella.

"Well, there are some things to avoid. You will need to use **adjectives** to describe things, but don't go overboard with techniques like **simile** or **metaphor**. It's fine to describe a dog as lively, but you wouldn't say he was a bundle of energy or like a bull in a china shop."

"I see. Not that any of those descriptions would be any good for Spotless at the moment anyway. Fat and lazy would be more like it!" laughed Isabella, prodding a disgruntled Spotless.

## Owning a dog
### Plan

### Introduction
This report is about what it is like to own a dog.

Owning a dog is hard work, but rewarding.

### Paragraph one
Choosing a puppy

- How big will it grow?
- Can you afford to keep it?
- Have you got time to exercise it?

### Paragraph two
Taking care of a dog

- Immunisations
- Exercise
- Feeding
- Training
- Grooming

### Conclusion
Owning a dog needs careful thought. They can be expensive to keep and need lots of time, but they are lots of fun.

## Top Tips
Aim to write one paragraph for each of your topics, plus one each for the introduction and conclusion.

## Did you know?
Non-chronological reports are about the way things are, not how you see them. So talk about what people *generally* think, rather than what *you* think.

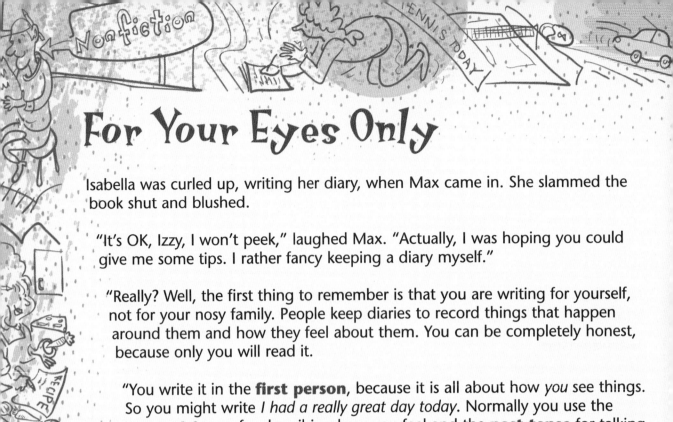

# For Your Eyes Only

Isabella was curled up, writing her diary, when Max came in. She slammed the book shut and blushed.

"It's OK, Izzy, I won't peek," laughed Max. "Actually, I was hoping you could give me some tips. I rather fancy keeping a diary myself."

"Really? Well, the first thing to remember is that you are writing for yourself, not for your nosy family. People keep diaries to record things that happen around them and how they feel about them. You can be completely honest, because only you will read it.

"You write it in the **first person**, because it is all about how *you* see things. So you might write *I had a really great day today*. Normally you use the **present tense** for describing how you feel and the **past tense** for talking about things that happened during the day. You can use informal language and creative techniques like **simile** and **metaphor** if you like, too," explained Isabella.

Can you keep a secret? My diary is hidden under the sofa.

"Do I have to write in it every day?" asked Max.

"Some people do, but if you do the same type of thing every day, it can get a bit boring. Other people just write an entry when something exciting or unusual happens. It's up to you."

"Thanks, Izzy. Keeping a diary sounds like fun. I think I'll start today!" said Max, excitedly.

Later that day, Isabella crept into the kitchen. There, on the table, was Max's diary.

"Well, a little look won't hurt," she said to herself. "Surely there can't be much of any interest for a butler to write about, anyway."

She was in for a surprise!

### Thursday 21 March

Got up at 7am, as usual. Made the breakfast, cleared away and took Spotless for his walk. On the way, I stopped to help a motorist with a flat tyre. Was surprised to discover the Prime Minister sitting in the back of the car. Had a quick chat about the state of the economy.

Got back and prepared lunch for the family before heading out again to meet the head of the secret service. Helped him to crack a new code being used by foreign spies. He thinks I'm in line for a medal, which is exciting.

Rescued a kitten from a tree and just got back home in time to finish the ironing and make dinner.

A rather quiet day.

## Top Tips

It makes sense to put events in chronological order, but avoid making your diary just a list of every tiny thing you have done all day.

## Did you know?

Some diaries are published for other people to read. The most famous is probably *The Diary of Anne Frank*, written while Anne was in hiding in Holland during World War II, and published after her death in a concentration camp.

# Bus Stop Bust-up

Sir Ralph was in a dreadful mood. The council had decided to make a new bus route right past the house, with a stop just outside.

"It will be so noisy, Izzy," complained Sir Ralph. "All the passengers will be waiting around outside the house. Not to mention all the pollution. The petunias won't like that, you know. Don't you think it's awful, Izzy?"

"Actually, I think it's a great idea," argued Isabella. "I'll be able to get the bus to school, or into town, without having to ask you for lifts, and if everyone used the bus instead of driving everywhere in their cars, there would be less pollution, not more. So you see, I'm right, and you're wrong!"

Max intervened. "There's no need to turn this into a big dispute. Let's write it all out, as a **balanced argument**, and see where that gets us. Balanced arguments set out the views on both sides, so people can read them and make up their own minds what they think. The introduction says what the argument is about and might mention a key fact about its importance. The new bus route has caused a big reaction in the local community, so we can put that in our introduction."

"OK, Max," said Sir Ralph. "Then we can have my two arguments against the bus route: the noise and the pollution. Then we'll follow that with Izzy's two points in its favour: the flexibility it will give people and her belief that overall it will reduce pollution. We can use **connectives** like *however, on the other hand, but* or *also*, to link the different points of view together."

"Fine," said Isabella, "but to make the arguments more convincing on both sides we need some evidence, perhaps from a scientific study or an opinion poll. There is some research in the local newspaper that we could use."

"Good," said Max. "Now all we need is a conclusion. Conclusions sum up the main points on each side of the debate, or suggest a third view.

"For example, while you two have been squabbling about the new route, I was on the phone to the council and they have agreed to move the bus stop a little further down the road, by the park. So we'll have all the convenience with none of the noise. What's more, the bus will have a fuel-efficient engine, so it really will be better for the environment. Now that's what I call a perfect conclusion!"

Whatever your own opinion, make sure your argument is balanced. Include two points for, and two against, and don't favour one view over the other in your introduction or conclusion.

## Did you know?

Newspaper reports are often written as balanced arguments. Try writing a newspaper report about the proposed bus route.

connectives

after, next, later

conclusion - draws the points together

factual descriptions

main report - one paragraph for each topic

structu

language

chronological order

introduction - what is it about?

include all the relevant info

structure

Chronological reports (recour

points in order

use numbers or letters

Structure

simple and clear

use address of person you are writing to

Language

INSTRUCTI

imperative verbs

start with why you are writing

structure

Formal

language

Jane Jones
24 The Street
New Town

LET

Informal

end with what you want to happen now

Dear Sir / Yours faithfully

Dear Mr Smith / Yours sincerely

structure

structure

language

introduction - what is the debate?

just your address

2 points for, 2 points against

start by asking how they are

Dear Kath...

see you soon, Ben

use evidenc

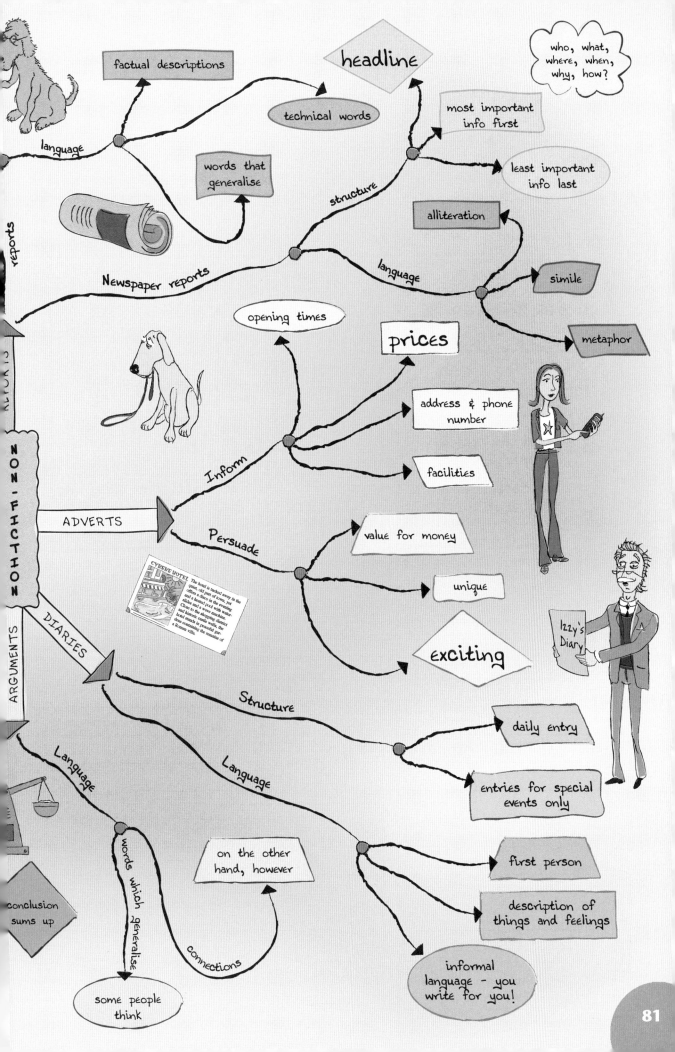

factual descriptions

headline

who, what, where, when, why, how?

technical words

most important info first

language

words that generalise

least important info last

structure

alliteration

reports

Newspaper reports

language

simile

metaphor

opening times

prices

address & phone number

Inform

facilities

ADVERTS

Persuade

value for money

unique

CYBELE HOTEL

exciting

DIARIES

Structure

daily entry

ARGUMENTS

Language

Language

entries for special events only

Izzy's Diary

Language

first person

words which generalise

on the other hand, however

description of things and feelings

conclusion sums up

connections

some people think

informal language – you write for you!

NON-FICTION

# Revise Time

**1 Put these instructions for making a cheese sandwich in the correct order, by numbering them 1 to 5.**

Spread butter on one side of each slice ☐

Put the second slice of bread on top, buttered side down ☐

Slice the sandwich in half ☐

Cut two slices of bread ☐

Grate some cheese onto the buttered side of one of the slices of bread ☐

**2 Read the recount below and rewrite it as a short newspaper report, complete with headline.**

It started to rain at 6pm last night. The river level continued to rise until it burst its banks at 10.30pm. When houses started to flood, the coastguard was called in to rescue people stranded by the water. After four hours, the water receded and the clean-up operation began.

_____

_____

_____

_____

_____

_____

_____

_____

_____

_____

_____

## 3

**Imagine you have written this diary entry. Write a short informal letter to a friend telling them about your day at the theme park.**

Saturday 8 August
   Got up really early to go to the theme park with Suzy. I was so excited I could hardly sleep last night.
   When we got there we couldn't decide which ride to go on first. We had to queue for some of them. I liked the Crazy Corkscrew best. We had chips for lunch and then went on more rides, until Suzy said she felt sick!

_____

_____

_____

_____

_____

_____

_____

## 4

**Read this non-chronological report, and use the information in it to write a passage for an advertising brochure for a new bowling alley. Make up any details about things like location, pricing or opening times that you need for your advert.**

Ten-pin Bowling

   Ten-pin bowling is a popular sport and new bowling alleys are opening all over the country.
   People like ten-pin bowling because the whole family can play together. Because it is indoors, it can be played in any weather.
   Players have to wear special shoes to protect the slippery bowling alley. Bowling balls are quite heavy but they come in smaller sizes for children. To play, you have to bowl the ball at ten skittles, called pins, at the end of the alley. Your score depends on how many you knock down.

_____

_____

_____

_____

_____

_____

_____

# Reading Booklet

### Beside the Seaside

### Introduction

Living on an island, the sea has always held a fascination for the British and this interest gave rise to a huge new industry in the nineteenth century as families escaped the grime of the cities for a day trip to the seaside.

*Taking the Air* describes Victorian seaside holidays, and you can read about one girl's first trip to the seaside in *New Horizons*.

### Taking the Air

Before the nineteenth century, taking holidays was the preserve of the wealthy. The rise of the middle classes and the arrival of the railways gave more families the opportunity to escape the overcrowded industrial towns and cities to the clean air of the coast. Initially most of these holidays were day trips. Hotels were exclusive and expensive, and few workers had paid holiday. But as the popularity of trips to the seaside increased, cheaper boarding houses opened, giving families the option of prolonging their stay.

Coastal air and swimming in the sea were believed by the Victorians to be good for the health, although Victorian modesty meant that men and women used separate beaches and bathing machines were used to enable swimmers to enter the water unseen. Like today, children enjoyed exploring the sand dunes and rock pools, and eating fish and chips and ice-cream.

The larger resorts, like Blackpool and Bournemouth, also offered an impressive array of theatres, variety halls and pleasure gardens to entertain visitors.

## New Horizons

Standing in the rain on the platform, hemmed in by the damp coats of the people around me, an unpleasant mixture of fear and excitement threatened to make me sick.

A dreadful hissing and grunting filled the air, like some huge demonic boar. Out of the dirty drizzle, the towering shape of the steam engine emerged. Bewildered, I felt myself led by the hand down the length of the train, that stretched like a serpent much further than I could see.

And then I was safe in the compartment, with the city blurred to a grey smudge as we shrugged off the grimy suburbs, to pop out, quite suddenly, into glossy green fields. Raised among a forest of chimneys, I had no idea that the world was so large.

Suddenly, between the rolling hills and dappled sky, was an expanse of brilliant, sparkling blue. It was the biggest thing I had ever seen, and I knew that it must be the sea.

# Section 1

These questions are about the report *Taking the Air*.

**Choose the best word or group of words to complete this sentence.**

1   Bathing machines were used:                                          *(1 mark)*

as cheap boarding houses ☐

to allow swimmers to enter the water unseen ☐

so that men and women could use the same beach ☐

to allow children to explore the rock pools ☐

2   **What gave Victorian families the option of prolonging their stay?** *(1 mark)*

_____

3   **Why were most holidays initially day trips?**                     *(1 mark)*

_____

_____

4   **Why was the title *Taking the Air* chosen for this text?**        *(2 marks)*

_____

_____

5   **List three things Victorian children liked to do at the beach.**  *(2 marks)*

_____

_____

6   **Why are the day trips described as an escape from the overcrowded industrial towns and cities?** *(3 marks)*

_____

_____

_____

_____

_____

# Section 2

These questions are about the fiction passage *New Horizons*.

1  **Why did the city blur to a 'grey smudge'?**                                                      *(1 mark)*

_____

_____

2  **Why does the child in the story feel an 'unpleasant mixture of fear and excitement'?**          *(1 mark)*

_____

_____

3  **Why does the child say that he or she did not know the world was so large?**                    *(1 mark)*

_____

_____

4  'A dreadful hissing and grunting filled the air, like some huge demonic boar.'

   **Why does the author use these words to describe how the train sounds to the child?**            *(2 marks)*

_____

_____

_____

5  'It was the biggest thing I had ever seen, and I knew that it must be the sea.'

   **How does the child recognise the sea?**                                                         *(2 marks)*

_____

_____

_____

6  **How do we know that the narrator in the story is a child? Give three reasons.**                 *(3 marks)*

_____

_____

_____

# Short Writing Paper

**Raging Rapids**

A new water park is opening in your town at the weekend, offering these facilities:

- Waterslides

- Hot tubs

- Wave machines

- Waterfalls

- Toddler pool

**Write an advertisement for the water park, to appear in a local newspaper.**

**Planning**

Key words to describe the facilities

_____

_____

_____

_____

_____

_____

_____

How the park will benefit the community

_____

_____

_____

_____

_____

_____

_____

_____

# Long Writing Paper

## Moving House

As we drew up outside our new house my heart sank. The curtainless windows stared down blankly. I was going to hate living here. Suddenly a face appeared over the garden wall. Maybe this wouldn't be so bad after all.

**Write a story based on this idea.**
**Think about:**

- the characters
- whose face appeared over the garden wall
- what happened next
- how your story will end

## Planning

Opening

_____

_____

_____

_____

_____

_____

Build-up

_____

_____

_____

_____

_____

_____

_____

**Dilemma**

_____
_____
_____
_____
_____
_____
_____

**Events**

_____
_____
_____
_____
_____
_____
_____
_____

**Resolution**

_____
_____
_____
_____
_____
_____
_____
_____

# Spelling Paper

There are some words missing from this piece of text about the plague. You will find the complete text on page 96. Ask a helper to read it to you, and fill in the missing words.

**The Black Death**

The Black Death was the _____ natural disaster _____ in the

Middle Ages. The plague first _____ in Europe in 1347. It was carried by

_____ rats who passed it on to humans _____ flea bites, and

people who became ill often _____ the same day.

The rats that _____ the plague lived in the _____ houses and

streets among the rubbish and dirt. They also lived on ships, carrying the

_____ from port to port. It took just 14 years for the plague to spread

from China to Britain.

The Black Death got its name from the black spots _____ developed.

Swellings also appeared in their armpits and _____, and some sufferers

_____ up _____. Medieval _____ did not know

how to _____ it, or where it came from.

People _____ their homes to escape the _____, but they took

the plague with them and the disease _____ across Europe. As many as

a third of the population of Europe died, leaving many villages deserted. It is

_____ that 25 million _____ died in Europe alone.

# Glossary

**abstract nouns** a concept or idea, e.g. *love, bravery*

**active verbs** describe who is doing the action, e.g. Ben *put* the books away

**adjective** a word or phrase added to a noun to add to or modify it. Comparative adjectives describe a degree of a quality, e.g. *more* happy, *taller*. Superlative adjectives describe the greatest extent of a quality, e.g. *biggest, most* or *least* expensive

**adverb** a word or phrase that adds to or modifies a verb. run *quickly, very* tired

**alliteration** a phrase where most or all of the words begin with the same sound, e.g. *Bonny babies bounce beautifully*

**apostrophe** a punctuation mark used for contraction, when two words are joined, or to show possession, e.g. *Don't take Mary's bag*

**balanced argument** a piece of non-fiction writing designed to explain opposing points of view. The writer does not favour one opinion over the other

**brackets** marks surrounding extra pieces of information. Their removal does not affect the meaning of the text

**chronological report** a piece of non-fiction writing recording events in the order in which they happened. Also called recounts

**clause** a distinct part of a sentence including a verb. The main clause is the main part of the sentence. It makes sense on its own. The subordinate clause adds extra information but does not make sense on its own. An embedded clause is placed in the middle of a sentence

**comma** shows when to pause, separates clauses, or separates items in a list

**collective nouns** name a group of people or things, e.g. *crowd of people, troupe of monkeys*

**comparative adjectives** describe a degree of a quality, e.g. *more* beautiful, *taller*

**complex sentences** contain a main clause and a subordinate clause

**compound sentences** contain two equally weighted clauses, joined together with a conjunction

**conjunction** a word used to link sentences or clauses, or to connect words within a phrase, e.g. *because, but, later*

**connective** word or phrase used to connect different parts of a text

**consonants** all the letters of the alphabet except the vowels a, e, i, o and u

**contraction** words which are shortened, or two words that are joined, by removing letters and replacing with an apostrophe

**direct speech** words actually spoken, enclosed in speech marks

**embedded clause** a clause that is placed in the middle of a sentence

**exclamation marks** can be used instead of full stops to indicate surprise or that an order has been made, e.g. *Hey! Stop that!*

**fiction** stories with imaginary characters, settings or events

**first person** text written as if from the writer's point of view, *e.g. I saw the car swerve towards me*

**future tense** describes what will or may happen in the future

**genre** a style or type of writing. Texts can belong to more than one genre, e.g. historical romance

**indent** to start a new paragraph slightly in from the end of a new line. The first paragraph in a text is not indented

**inference and deduction** when the reader uses their own knowledge, and the imagery created by the author, to read beyond the explicit meaning of the text

**main clause** is the main part of the sentence. It makes sense on its own

**metaphor** where a writer describes something as if it were something else, e.g. *he's a loose canon*

**mnemonic** a memorable phrase that helps you remember spelling patterns

**non-fiction** writing that is not fiction, including information texts about real people and places, letters, instructions and reports

**noun** a word that names a thing or feeling.
abstract nouns name a concept or idea, e.g. *love, bravery*
collective nouns name a group of people or things, e.g. *crowd of people, troupe of monkeys*
common nouns names ordinary things, e.g. *cat*
proper nouns describe a specific person, thing or place, e.g. *Kyle, London, Tuesday*

**onomatopoeia** words which sound like the noise they describe, e.g. *plop, rustle, crunch*

**paragraph** a section of a piece of writing. New paragraphs signal a change in topic, place or time, or that a new person is speaking. (see also indent)

**passive verbs** describe the action, e.g. The books *were put* away by Ben

**past tense** describes things which have happened

**personification** a writing technique in which human characteristics are used to describe non-human things, e.g. The branches of the tree reached out to us

**phrase** two or more words that act as a unit

**plural** more than one of something. Usually made by adding s, es, or ies, e.g. *cars, bushes, babies*. There are some exceptions, e.g. *people, children*

**prefix** a group of letters added to the beginning of a word to change its meaning, e.g. *unhappy, disobedient*

**present tense** describes things which are happening now

**pronoun** a word used instead of a noun to avoid having to use the same noun again, e.g. *he, you, my, that*

**punctuation** marks added to writing to make it easier to understand.
**apostrophes** are punctuation marks used for contraction, when two words are joined, or to show possession, e.g. *Don't take Mary's bag*
**brackets** surround extra pieces of information. Their removal does not affect the meaning of the text
**commas** show when to pause, separate clauses, or separate items in a list
**full stops** mark the end of sentences, although question marks are used for questions,

and exclamation marks to indicate surprise or that an order has been made
**speech marks** surround direct speech. Other punctuation goes inside them

**question marks** can be used in place of a full stop to show that a question has been asked

**recount** a chronological report

**reported speech** speech reported in a text, but not directly quoted, e.g. *He said he would be late*

**root word** a word that you can add a prefix or suffix to

**scan** to read quickly to find a specific piece of information

**sentence** a unit of text that makes sense on its own.
**simple sentences** contain only one clause
**compound sentences** contain two equally weighted clauses, joined together with a conjunction
**complex sentences** contain a main clause and a subordinate clause

**simile** where a writer compares something to something else, e.g. *as clean as a whistle, sleeping like a baby*

**simple sentences** contain only one clause

**singular** one of something, e.g. *a dog, the girl*

**skim** to read quickly to understand the main meaning of a text

**speech marks** surround direct speech. Other punctuation goes inside them, e.g. *"Hello!" said Ian*

**subordinate clause** adds extra information but does not make sense on its own, e.g. The cat, *which was ginger*, leapt onto the wall

**suffix** a group of letters added to the end of a root word to change its meaning, e.g. *helpless, boldly*

**superlative adjectives** describe the extent of a quality, e.g. the *biggest, the most or least expensive*

**synonyms** words with the same or similar meanings, e.g. *cold, chilly*

**tense** tells us when something is happening.
**past tense** describes things which have happened
**present tense** describes things which are happening now
**future tense** describes what will or may happen

**thesaurus** a book of synonyms

**verb** doing or being words.
**active verbs** describe who is doing the action, e.g. Ben *put* the books away.
**imperative verbs** give an order or instruction, e.g. Take a piece of paper.
**irregular verbs** do not add the standard ed in the past tense. Instead, their past tense form changes completely, e.g. I go, I went, I bring, I brought.
**passive verbs** describe the action, e.g. The books *were put* away by Ben

**vowels** a, e, i, o and u. The other letters in the alphabet are consonants

**word family** groups of words that share the same root, prefix or suffix

# Answers

## Pages 28–29 Revision exercises

### Exercise 1

The correct spellings are:

a shameful    e dared
b skiing    f raking
c hungrily    g graceful
d tried    h lovely

```
h  u  p  g  a  e  v  w  k  h
l  o  v  i  d  e  r  v  s  u
e  w  g  r  a  d  d  w  l  n
m  o  h  g  r  a  k  i  n  g
r  e  q  s  e  l  n  d  e  r
t  r  i  e  d  p  k  l  e  i
i  r  s  h  a  m  e  f  u  l
y  h  k  t  c  k  w  e  l  y
b  r  i  w  q  a  l  f  y  o
u  t  i  t  e  w  d  l  j  p
f  t  n  r  a  d  e  h  i  l
w  s  g  r  a  c  e  f  u  l
l  o  v  e  l  y  i  i  n  d
h  r  y  l  f  e  b  s  w  q
```

### Exercise 2

Jack came into the room. "Hello Ben," he said. "Are you nearly finished?"

Ben looked up from his homework. "It's pretty difficult, but I'm nearly there."

"Great!" exclaimed Jack. "Then we can play football."

### Exercise 3

Many different descriptions are possible. A good one will use past tense verbs. Appropriate words to use from the box would be: short, green, she, skirt and trainers.

### Exercise 4

Sentences may vary, but typical complex sentences might be:

a I left my bag, which was blue, on the bus.
b After tea, I went swimming.
c I went to Spain, for my holiday.

### Exercise 5

a F
b T
c T
d F
e T
f T

## Pages 42–43 Revision exercises

### Exercise 1

The correct answer is B.

### Exercise 2

The film was successful because:
It had a first class script
Of the computer-generated special effects
Of the great cast

### Exercise 3

A modern take on a classic story means bringing an old, classic story up to date by giving it a modern setting.

### Exercise 4

Simon Sealberg doesn't want to give away any secrets about the script for the sequel, because if he did, the story wouldn't be a surprise any more, so people might not want to see the film.

### Exercise 5

Because the author thinks the sound of the sea washing in and out is similar to the steady rhythmical sound of the heartbeat of a huge animal.

### Exercise 6

The sound of the sea always lulls Molly to sleep because it is a soothing, rhythmical sound with which Molly is familiar.

### Exercise 7

The unknown threat in the caves is the pirates. We know because of the title of the extract, and because of the pirate tales we hear about in the first paragraph.

### Exercise 8

Swish and sway is a good description of the way the sea washes in and out. It is alliteration too, and the s sound at the beginning of both words also sounds like the sea.

## Pages 62–63 Revision exercises

### Exercise 1

Good character notes will cover appearance and personality, the relationship between the characters, and even the kinds of things they might say.

### Exercise 2

Think about any special adjectives or adverbs you want to use, and consider using simile, metaphor or alliteration. Personification also works well for describing settings.

### Exercise 3

A good opening sets the scene and introduces your characters. Think how you want to start: with a description of the setting, a character, or with dialogue? Also think about the genre you are writing.

### Exercise 4

A good cliffhanger ending leaves questions unanswered, or may leave a character in peril. You want your reader to think on about what might happen next. Make sure you have left clues about possible outcomes earlier in the story, but don't be too obvious.

## Page 82–83 Revision exercises

### Exercise 1

The correct order is 2, 4, 5, 1, 3

### Exercise 2

A good answer will include information about what happened, when and where, as well as why it happened and who was involved. Strong answers will start with the key information, with less important facts lower down. A good headline will sum up the story in a few words and may use alliteration or another creative technique for impact.

### Exercise 3

A good answer will use an appropriate layout for an informal letter, ie sender's address, date, Dear (first name). It should open with a greeting, use friendly and informal language, and end with a friendly message, signed with the sender's first name only.

### Exercise 4

A good answer will persuade the reader that the bowling alley is exciting and good value for money. Superlative or comparative adjectives may be used. Strong answers will strike a balance between persuading and informing, including details of opening times, prices and location.

## Reading booklet

### Section 1

1 Bathing machines were used to allow swimmers to enter the water unseen.

2 Cheaper boarding houses

3 Because hotels were expensive and few people had paid holiday.

4 Because the air at the coast was much cleaner than in the cities, and was one of the reasons people went to the seaside.

5 Any three from:

Exploring sand dunes

Exploring rock pools

Eating fish and chips

Eating ice-creams

6 A good answer will recognise that the cities were unpleasant, dirty places to be, and that the seaside was seen as a clean, healthy alternative.

### Section 2

1 A good answer will describe the blurring of the view from a fast train, and link the colour grey to the grime of the city.

2 A good answer will talk about the fear of the crowds and the train as seen from a child's perspective, and the excitement of going on the train and seeing the sea, and will recognise that this conflicting mix would feel physically unpleasant.

3 A good answer will spot that because the child was raised among a forest of chimneys, he or she may not have left the city or seen open spaces before.

4 A good answer will spot that this is personification, used to show how the huge train seems in the imagination of the small child.

5 A good answer will suggest that although the child has never seen the sea, he or she knows that it is water and will be the biggest thing he or she has ever seen, so when the child spots the huge expanse of water, he or she guesses that it must be the sea.

6 Good answers would be:

The child is hemmed in by the coats of people on the platform, so must be much shorter than the people around him or her.

The child is led by the hand down the platform, and that is something that usually happens to a child.

The steam engine towers above the narrator, again suggesting that he or she must be short.

### Short writing paper

A good answer will persuade the reader that the water park is exciting and offers a good range of activities for everyone. Superlative or comparative adjectives may be used. Strong answers will strike a balance between persuading and informing, including details of opening times, prices and location. Strong answers will also focus on the benefits to the local community.

### Long writing paper

Strong answers will have a good range of short and more complex sentences with correct punctuation. The storyline will be well developed so that the story is convincing, and the writing will use a variety of creative devices, e.g. metaphor, simile, personification and techniques to draw the reader in and hold their interest.

### Spelling paper

The Black Death

The Black Death was the worst natural disaster seen in the Middle Ages. The plague first appeared in Europe in 1347. It was carried by infected rats who passed it on to humans through flea bites, and people who became ill often died the same day.

The rats that carried the plague lived in the overcrowded houses and streets among the rubbish and dirt. They also lived on ships, carrying the disease from port to port. It took just 14 years for the plague to spread from China to Britain.

The Black Death got its name from the black spots sufferers developed. Swellings also appeared in their armpits and groin, and some sufferers coughed up blood. Medieval doctors did not know how to cure it, or where it came from.

People fled their homes to escape the infection, but they took the plague with them and the disease spread across Europe. As many as a third of the population of Europe died, leaving many villages deserted. It is estimated that 25 million people died in Europe alone.